Tomorrow's KM:
Innovation, best practice, and the future of knowledge management

EDITED BY ALEX DAVIES

Commissioning editor
Alex Davies

Published by
Globe Law and Business Ltd
3 Mylor Close
Horsell
Woking
Surrey GU21 4DD
United Kingdom
Tel: +44 20 3745 4770
www.globelawandbusiness.com

ISBN: 978-1-78358-374-4
A catalogue record for this book is available from the British Library

Contents

Executive summary

Innovation is arguably an integral part of the knowledge management function and KM practice – as a popular "buzzword" over the past few years, and in the fast changing business world of today, it has become the mainstay of professional service organizations. The complexity of innovation increases with the growth in knowledge available to organizations, and with this comes the need to determine its place in business.

Tomorrow's KM: Innovation, best practice, and the future of knowledge management focuses on the relationship between innovation and KM, elaborating on the role of KM as the facilitator and enabler of change. Consisting of in depth case studies and insight from experts within varied fields, this book offers some contextual trendspotting and a general overview of the market.

In order to "innovate", one needs to know what it actually means. What is innovation and how does it relate to KM? Where does it start and end within the organization? How do you find out what you need to know in order to innovate? In the book's opening chapter, Hélène Russell of TheKnowledgeBusiness defines what innovation means in relation to KM, setting the tone for the rest of the contributions. Helene then goes on to explore the nature of diversity in KM. It is thought that one important way to improving innovative thought within organizations is to break silos and increase the opportunities for those of different backgrounds and knowledge to interact. Hélène explores the evidence and offers practical ideas to improve opportunities for innovation to arise in this way.

The next chapter looks at where KM "sits" within the organization. In the past, when knowledge management initiatives revolved around the gathering and organization of internal precedents or the implementation of specific technology such as a SharePoint portal or enterprise search, the knowledge manager or the knowledge management department had more control over the success of the initiative. With today's emphasis on practice innovation to position a law firm for financial success and lawyer retention, today and in the future, successful initiatives are rarely the result of work by one person or one department; success or failure depends on the engagement of multiple departments and individuals. Chapter two by Cyndi Murphy, knowledge manager at Stewart McKelvey, focuses on specific examples that demonstrate the need for practice innovation to be embraced, implemented, and shared across an organization.

Chapter three looks at how the role of the knowledge manager will change to reflect wider field transformation. What new capabilities will they need to develop? What people will you need to be looking for in the future? Data scientists who can provide insights and analysis; those who can tell a story with data? Raymond Olayinka, senior advisory consultant at Arup, suggests that the role of KM will increasingly suit those who are more proactive than reactive, moving away from those who can maintain systems to those who can engage stakeholders and bridge practice and knowledge.

If innovation is dispersed across an organization, KM – as a department with a finger in multiple pies – is in the perfect position to own it and pull the various threads from different departments together. How is this achieved? What can be done to facilitate collaboration between different functions and initiatives? In chapter four, Sara Traynor of Sara Traynor Coaching gives an overview of a project used to pioneer knowledge management collaboration in a south west UK law firm, the purpose of which was for lawyers to collaborate, share knowledge, and learn from each other.

While innovation is the engine of an industry and a society, organizations can sometimes struggle to innovate or invent in a sustained manner. It continues to be an esoteric art, a mystery, and innovators are revered across organizations and industry. In chapter five, Randhir Pushpa, founder and chief consultant, ACIES Innovations, maintains that despite extensive research work, we are still not able to change innovating into a science. With innovation, we do not have the control that we have with other activities in an organization, and whilst we may be confident in planning and then dominating a particular market, we will not have the same confidence in planning and innovating in a particular technology. One of the reasons has been because researchers in innovation are not ready to admit or accept that innovation is nothing but new knowledge. Probably an admission may lessen the mystery around innovating, and push it down from the pedestal on which it is kept. Art has to move to science, if it has to be practiced, controlled, and sustained. The science behind innovating in a sustained manner is still in the nascent stage, and this chapter argues that the reason is because we are not ready to explore innovation by removing all the laces and frills it is packaged with. An approach to sustained innovation is shared, along with a case study.

The workplace is changing – different kinds of working and multiple locations mean that new ways of sharing and exchanging knowledge need to be negotiated. The millennial isn't just inheriting the earth; as it comes of age it is fundamentally redesigning the workplace. Alongside the arrival of this first generation of genuinely tech-savvy workers, a revolution is gathering steam. It isn't just about flexing the bricks and mortar of office space, or even installing IOT-enabled connected furnishings. Demands for different kinds of flexible working, across multiple locations, have given a new centricity to knowledge management within firms keen to ensure the efficient sharing and retaining of their corporate's learning, as well as its talent. While millennials work differently, they also communicate differently. Finding innovative KM strategies for this brave new world, ways that respond most effectively to Industry 4.0 and its demand for data-driven digital platforms, will prove key to future survival. In chapter six, Clare Harman Clark, senior professional support lawyer at Taylor Wessing, looks at how to share knowledge in the future workplace.

Chapter seven looks at what KM should actually *do*. Should KM be focused on the capture and sharing of knowledge, or could it create greater opportunities by designing, developing, and delivering processes, structure, and behavior related to stimulating learning and optimizing processes for harnessing knowledge as it emerges? If KM sits at the hub of the organizational wheel and its potential impact on operational effectiveness and people, it should be part of the mechanism of and for change. How do we do that? It has to start with how KM feeds into innovation. Caroline White-Robinson, head of L&D at Shoosmiths, argues the case for knowledge and its related management to be "just-in-time" and emergent.

Communities of Practices (CoPs) have proven to be a very powerful KM practice to manage and to leverage knowledge domains in organizations, particularly for organizational learning and problem-solving issues. CoPs can also turn into the innovation engine of organizations by also playing the role of Communities of Innovation (CoIs). In chapter eight, Vincent Ribiere, managing director and co-founder of the Institute for Knowledge and Innovation Southeast Asia discusses how CoPs and CoIs allow knowledge and ideas to flow internally in the organization, as well as communicate and collaborate with external communities to slowly build innovation ecosystems.

About the authors

Clare Harman Clark is a senior professional support lawyer at Taylor Wessing LLP, building on a legal career that began over a decade ago at Clifford Chance. Before retraining as a lawyer, Clare worked as a journalist and within a government press office, and still regularly publishes articles in national and trade press. She has also been appointed as a guest lecturer in property law at the University of Westminster.

Cyndi Murphy is the knowledge manager in the Halifax office of Stewart McKelvey. Her firm-wide responsibilities include liaising with practice groups and administrative departments for the successful implementation of knowledge management projects, overseeing content management of the internal SharePoint portal and various internal databases, and attending meetings of the practice innovation advisory committee. An honored member and past president of the Canadian Association of Law Libraries (CALL), she is actively involved in the knowledge management and private law libraries special interest groups, as well as serving on the copyright committee. Cyndi has participated in a number of CALL conference panel presentations on knowledge management and other topics. In 2017, she spoke on "Matter-Centric Knowledge Management" at the ARK KM conference held in New York, and contributed to the ARK publication, *Innovations in Legal KM.*

Raymond Olayinka is a senior advisory consultant at Arup and subject matter expert in helping client organizations to develop and deploy knowledge management strategies. He started his career in civil engineering and successfully worked as project engineer and project manager on building projects. Raymond began his work on knowledge management in 2006 and has since held specialist roles with various organizations. He offers a wealth of knowledge management expertise gained through delivering projects in energy, infrastructure, transport, education, and international development. He has led, developed, and overseen knowledge and learning initiatives at corporate level, working in partnership with various stakeholders. His current interest is in the optimization of organizational knowledge to improve business performance through the development of knowledge management systems and programs.

Dr Randhir Reghunath Pushpa is a knowledge and innovation management consultant and researcher. His main focus is to evolve KM as a practice that can bring tangible benefits to organizations. He does work on leveraging knowledge and improving sales, automation, and cost cutting. In innovation management he has been involved in setting up innovation eco-systems, which can help in sustained innovation. At Unisys Bangalore, he set up an innovation program focusing on patent productivity, which resulted in a spurt in innovation in a sustained manner. He is the chief consultant and founder of Acies Innovations (a knowledge and innovation consulting firm). He works very closely with Knowledge Management Society Singapore and is also a member of KM Global Network. He writes regularly on next generation knowledge management. His areas of interest include knowledge management, innovation management, artificial intelligence, and human–machine collaboration.

Dr Vincent Ribiere is an enthusiastic and creative international consultant and professor with a passion for helping organizations solve their organizational knowledge and innovation management challenges. He is the founder and managing director of the Institute for Knowledge and Innovation Southeast Asia (IKI-SEA), a center of excellence at Bangkok University, as well as the program director of the Ph.D. in KM and Innovation Management. He has also co-founded various internationals events in the fields of business creativity and innovation (Creative Bangkok, ASCIM, CreativeMornings Bangkok, G-LINK) and co-founded various communities of KM and innovation academics and practitioners nationally (iKlub, Thai KM Network) and internationally (KM Global Network). Vincent has a strong entrepreneurial spirit and enjoys sharing his knowledge and experiences. He delivers keynote speeches and workshops at various international professional and academic conferences and is the author of more than 80 publications.

Hélène Russell of TheKnowledgeBusiness is a lawyer (non-practicing) and specialist in KM. After working in clinical negligence litigation defense work for eight years, then two years in an in-house KM team, she has worked as a self-employed KM consultant since 2008.

Hélène specializes in translating complex academic thought leadership and cross-boundary theories into practical tools to improve the efficiency and profitability of real-life law firms. She focuses on producing practical textbooks, hands-on workshops and giving independent advice. She particularly enjoys helping those firms that have reached a tipping point and need practical help with their first major knowledge audit and strategy, but she has helped large and small firms alike.

Hélène is the author of *Knowledge Management Handbook*, published by the Law Society of England and Wales, *Practical Projects in Legal KM*, published by Legal Monitor, and is a contributor to ARK's *Measuring the ROI of KM, 2nd Edition*, *Innovations in Legal KM*, *Emerging approaches to law firm profitability*, and *The Changing Role of the Professional Support Lawyer*.

Her book *Practical Projects in Legal KM* was declared "clear, succinct, jargon-free and one of the most pragmatic KM texts I have come across … Anyone dealing with legal KM should have a copy of this book. It's as simple as that," by head of client knowledge and learning at Linklaters, Ian Rodwell.

She has spoken at various events, including Lexpo Legal Innovation conference, ARK's KM Legal, Butterworth's PSL conference, and for UWE, BLS and Allice. She runs regular open KM training events in London, KM community groups nationwide under the "Knowledge Network UK" brand, and bespoke in-house training. She has completed an executive MBA with distinction, studying antecedents to knowledge sharing within UK law firms for her dissertation.

Sara Traynor is an executive and leadership coach specializing in coaching lawyers transitioning to board roles or heads of department. She also coaches groups and teams using the globally renowned LEGO serious play methodology and is the only certified facilitator in south west England. Sara was previously the director of knowledge and learning at Stephens Scown LLP, a *Times* Top 100 Best Companies to Work For. Sara pioneered the firm's KM strategy, which focused on lawyers sharing knowledge and learning from each other. Previously, Sara worked at a FTSE 250 utility for 15 years with management roles in organizational development, change management, service delivery, and project management.

Caroline White-Robinson is head of knowledge management and learning and development at Shoosmiths. Knowledge management is a function that aims to bring all tacit and explicit knowledge within Shoosmiths together in a consistent way, complementing the learning and development area where Caroline has headed up the team for the last ten years. The overall strategy is to equip everyone in Shoosmiths with the necessary knowledge and skills to be able to fulfil their role. Caroline's passion is leadership development, strategy development, and helping people find their way in the business world. Having studied for various qualifications for most of her adult life, Caroline uses her experience to find pragmatic solutions for the challenges in today's world. She is proud to lead a team who are passionate about what they do.

Chapter 1:
Innovation, creativity, and knowledge

By Hélène Russell, TheKnowledgeBusiness

We are in unfamiliar territory. Sectors once thought to be stable, such as accountancy and law, are now struggling. Professions can no longer rely on the "information gap" and must offer clients more value than that contained within traditional services. Employers are struggling to understand the current generation, which is well educated but doesn't act or engage like previous ones. We are seeing new styles of businesses such as Netflix, Uber, and Airbnb, which are reinventing how services are delivered, and we anticipate considerable role disruption as Artificial Intelligence (AI) threatens many aspects of service delivery. Everything appears to be changing more quickly.

At times such as these, many organizations turn to "innovation" – but what does this mean and where and how should they start?

What is "innovation"?

"Innovation" is a deceptively simple term but is unfortunately used by people to mean many different things.

Whether you are finding ways to improve partnership profits in delivering legal services in competitive times, finding new "blue ocean" markets for services, or finding effective ways to deliver legal information and help to the most needy in society who have no means to pay, getting to grips with what is meant by "innovation" can help significantly in the first steps to understanding how to create a more innovative organization.

If asked for an innovation definition, Google is less than helpful, offering over 300 million results with thousands of definitions. Its own definition is pretty unhelpful too: "The action or process of innovating". Traditional sources such as the *Oxford English Dictionary* are a little more help – "Make changes in something established, especially by introducing new methods, ideas, or products" – but this is perhaps too simple to be of use to organizations.

Fundamentally, innovation is a process that involves multiple activities to uncover new ways to do things. It is about putting new ideas or approaches into action to provide new value. Innovations can be big or small; they can be breakthrough/disruptive or they can be incremental and build on existing products or services. They are usually useful and often surprising.

Innovation is often confused with "invention", which is the creation of something entirely new. Innovation is not just about "the big new idea" but about an idea that creates or adds value in some way, which is then put into practice. We must also separate "innovation" from "creation", which is the transdisciplinary process of bringing something into being.

Innovation involves both invention and creation but is different to both. Clearly, if an organization fails to distinguish between these terms, it could miss opportunities to capitalize on its creations or fail to invest in smaller innovations because they lack novelty.

Innovation can come in many forms but generally falls into two categories:

- Product/service innovation:
  - Developing entirely new and improved products and services. This may be to meet rapidly changing customer or consumer demands or needs, or to create new markets; or
  - Adding value to existing products, services, or markets to differentiate the business from its competitors and increase the perceived value to the customers; and
- Process innovation:
  - Improving or replacing business processes to increase efficiency and productivity, or to enable the business to extend the range or quality of existing products and/or services.

Although innovations are often primarily considered within the context of business and competition, they aren't necessarily about creating profit. Innovation is about creating new value as defined by the user, customer, or market, and innovative services could be provided pro bono or at low cost to customers who are unable to afford traditional services.

Why do organizations need innovation?

People buy solutions to their needs. They don't want a hammer; they want a hook in the wall for their picture to hang on in order to improve how their hallway looks. Clients don't want "a lawyer", they want a solution to a problem that concerns the law. Organizations that fail to understand this tend to fail to adapt to changing needs or to deliver solutions to those needs in a better, cheaper, more effective and innovative way.

Innovation helps established businesses compete, particularly against more agile start-ups. The barriers and hurdles that might once have prevented new entrants to markets are currently falling away. Start-ups now have better access to finance, easier and cheaper access to new technologies, and a globalized connectivity that enables people to collaborate across traditional boundaries and to find more easily the right partners and support. Organizations that invest in innovation are less likely to lose market share to those hungrier to identify new opportunities and better methods to solve current problems and deliver value to customers.

In addition, innovating also helps to motivate and ground employees in the mission and values of the organization, or perhaps to question and improve that mission, and helps all stakeholders to focus on the value that they deliver, rather than becoming side-tracked into the detail of delivery of existing products and services.

How do innovations come to fruition?

Innovation requires an organization to:

- Challenge the status quo;
- Have a deep understanding of customers or users; and
- Develop imaginative solutions to how customer/user needs might be met.

Innovation is a messy, non-linear, creative process and ideas may come from inside the organization (employees, in-house designers, sales staff) or outside (suppliers, customers, market research, partnerships with local universities etc.). Organizations that ignore either route can miss the opportunities for new innovations.

Dorothy Leonard's book *When Sparks Fly* suggests there are five stages in the creative development of a suitable idea for innovation:

1. Preparation – when group members are selected to maximize creativity;
2. Innovation opportunity – when the group identifies the real problem requiring creativity;

3. Generation of options – when the group uses divergent thinking to produce many creative options;
4. Incubation – when the group takes time to analyze the various options; and
5. Convergence on one option – when the group moves from many options to one innovation that is then realized, marketed, and sold to customers or users.

Each team member is likely to have a natural preference for one or two aspects of the innovation process, but by being aware of these stages, team members can avoid becoming too frustrated with progress in areas that don't match their natural preferences.

Where does "knowledge" fit with innovation?

Key components of innovation are creative problem solving and the development of new ideas. But where does this creativity and novelty come from?

Research suggests that diverse teams – those that bring together different "knowledge" – are more creative and successful than even expert sole practitioners. This is true in academic fields such as mathematics, which have historically been dominated by lone geniuses, and in professional services businesses.

Before we explore why having different "knowledge" leads to innovation, it is necessary to clarify what we mean by "knowledge".

What is knowledge?

"Knowledge" is an intangible and diverse asset. It is broader, deeper, and richer than data or information. It is a mix of experiences, learning, values, contextual information, and insight. It is something beyond information upon which wise decisions can be based. In the legal sector, for example, a law, rule or regulation contains information, but a precedent, which enables lawyers to apply the law efficiently and effectively to solve a client's problem, contains knowledge.

Knowledge isn't a singular concept but exists on a spectrum. At one extreme, it is straightforward in nature and easily explained in words and can be distilled into and learned from documents, textbooks, diagrams, and precedents (known as explicit knowledge). At the other extreme, it is impossible to verbalize but informs decision-making and tactics and is learned through experiences (often described as tacit knowledge).

It can also be helpful to understand knowledge as both a stock that may be contained in books, precedents, and learning materials, and a flow, which is passed through conversation.

As we all grow, learn, and develop, both at work and at home, we continuously add to our internal knowledge stock – we learn things traditionally through lectures, research, and reading, and experientially. Sometimes we recognize our experiential learning through reflection and sometimes we don't realize what we've learned until we need to apply it in another situation.

This combined knowledge is a considerable asset for organizations, but, as you can imagine, people who are siloed within business units or departments can often end up with very similar "knowledge stocks".

Knowledge, diversity, and creative abrasion

Diversity supports innovation in two main ways. Firstly, diversity provides a greater pool of knowledge stocks for an organization. Secondly, diversity creates "creative abrasion".

"Creative abrasion" is a term coined by Jerry Hirshberg, founder and president of Nissan Design International and further developed by Dorothy Leonard in *Wellsprings of Knowledge* and *When Sparks Fly*. It occurs as those with different knowledge stocks are required to understand and learn from each other and re-evaluate their assumptions and heuristics/rules of thumb. It is the natural intellectual disagreement, questions, and discussions that occur when people with diverse backgrounds, knowledge, experiences, talents, cultures, and skillsets come together to work on business challenges, when ideas rub against each other productively as opposed to destructively.

Creative abrasion doesn't just occur when those of differing *technical* know-how interact. That diversity can come from different knowledge of brands, customer relationships, manufacturing processes, and service delivery capabilities, different skills, values, or ideas.

When employees from different departments or business units work together, or outsiders are recruited for the team, there is a natural collision of ideas. It is essential for successful problem framing and creative ideation phases as groups with similar knowledge tend to produce routine solutions, reusing familiar solutions. A more homogeneous group can be useful for the implementation/realization phase of new ideas.

Although "creative abrasion" is the common label for this creative clash of personal knowledge stocks, I wonder if "abrasion" perhaps suggests the wrong message about this process. This collision of knowledge stocks within individuals needn't cause disagreement or difficulty. With the right participants, it should be more about intellectual curiosity and exploration than disagreement, although perhaps "abrasion" is a useful reminder that the process needs careful management to avoid disharmony.

Often organizations use diverse teams from inside their businesses, combining those who serve different client sectors and those who undertake work that is technically different. However, including those from outside the organization as well can dramatically improve innovative thinking. Outsiders and new starters can more easily question conventions and encourage people to re-examine their jargon or assumptions, and reassess the standard solutions they usually reach for. Outsiders naturally challenge "the way things are done around here" because they have a different knowledge stock and mindset that has been created by working at different organizations. Outsiders and those new to a field can ask the kinds of questions insiders never would, the "This might be a stupid question but why...?" queries that are often surprisingly insightful as they tend to contain no underlying assumptions.

Often it won't be cost-effective for organizations to create a diverse work group for all business challenges touching upon innovations. It can be helpful, therefore, to consider the complexity and diversity of the problem faced by the business or the level of innovation sought and then bring a similar level of complexity and diversity to bear on the challenge.

How can businesses manage "creative abrasion" successfully?

Disagreement as a result of diverse viewpoints can be a challenging situation to manage, but it must be successfully managed if an organization is to produce a useful and valuable innovation.

A focus on intellectual curiosity and a learning mindset can help, as can:

- Communicating clearly to all parties that the diversity and disagreement is intentional and an asset;
- Finding some common ground;
- Using a bridge-manager;
- Taking a personalized approach; and
- Creating clear rules for engagement.

Firstly, for successful creative abrasion to occur, whilst there must be diversity as we've already seen, the group can't be so diverse that there is no common ground at all. Without at least some common areas of values, knowledge, or approach, there would be a complete lack of understanding of each other's knowledge stocks and mindsets, which would be difficult to overcome.

Secondly, the organization cannot assume the group can magically overcome their differences and collaborate and create together. The diverse group must be managed by someone with appropriate skills who can act as a bridge and help them work together and to trust and respect each other, and to keep differences to intellectual curiosity and handle any personal conflicts.

Thirdly, the bridge-manager must encourage the team to spend time understanding other team members' needs, preferences, and culture. Where an organization has a global workforce this is particularly important, as there may be strong cultural influences in play that can lead to frustrations and misunderstandings.

Lastly, before working together, the group, encouraged by the bridge-manager, will need to agree rules for collaborating. These needn't be complex but should focus on the need to be open and honest, and the need to discuss different thinking in a respectful way. It is always appropriate in an innovation team to be curious and ask questions, but all discussions should be the product of intellectual curiosity, with no personalized disagreements permitted, or, indeed, disagreements that aren't backed by data or clear knowledge-based reasoning. It can also be useful to agree in advance the limits to divergent and convergent thinking phases, so that no one becomes frustrated in those phases that don't suit their natural preferences.

How else can strategic management of knowledge and learning help organizations innovate?

Strategic management of knowledge and learning can also help organizations innovate by optimizing easy access to the explicit knowledge that its employees develop and share, and supporting and encouraging the flow of experiential and tacit knowledge between knowledgeable individuals, whatever team, department, or sector they are formally assigned to. In particular, they can try to break silos for learning and other events that cross boundaries, so that, say, negotiation or project management skills are learned in cross-disciplinary groups, building networks and opportunities for informal creative abrasion.

Informal networks (such as communities of practice, further explored in chapter eight) can also play an important part in sharing knowledge in unexpected ways and promoting novel thinking. Similarly, secondments and managed experiential learning programs, such as those discussed in Leonard's *Critical Knowledge Transfer*, can expose people within the organization to a wide variety of knowledge.

Lastly, organizations need to focus not only on hiring those with the requisite skills, but also those who are open to change, keen to learn and share their knowledge, those who are willing to network and include an element of cognitive diversity, and leaders need to pair/group people accordingly.

Innovation barriers and overcoming common mistakes

The most common mistake made by organizations wishing to improve innovation levels is hiring in and setting up a separate "innovation team" that is divorced from frontline employees.

Designated separate innovation teams permit frontline workers to feel that the task of "innovating" has been delegated. This can even, in more extreme circumstances, cause "innovation wars", when animosity between separate innovation teams and frontline workers becomes destructive for both, with the former disparaging the latter as bureaucratic, staid, and rigid and the latter disparaging the former as lacking discipline or accountability, with no one working in a constructive way. For successful innovation, organizations must create teams of different backgrounds from frontline experts who work together with mutual respect and curiosity. Organizations must balance strong messaging that innovation is everyone's responsibility to support the success and longevity of the organization, but also resist creating a glamour team and failing to laud and appreciate everyday work. Both need to be celebrated.

Another common mistake that organizations make in trying to boost innovation levels is to misunderstand the part that the customer must play. The innovation partner is indeed the customer and innovations are generally best co-produced with customers, but organizations must not stifle themselves with limited ideas of who customers might be, what their needs are, or what those customers value. If organizations focus solely on existing customers or rely on conventional market research, they will generally only be successful at improving on what already exists. This may enable incremental innovation but will not facilitate breakthrough innovations. Organizations need to build better conversational relationships with existing and potential customers to truly understand their needs, values, and thinking.

Another common mistake is a failure to understand and manage the whole process of innovation. Without sufficient investment, a clear vision of innovation's importance within the organization, an implementation plan, and management of the process, an organization can end up too focused on ideation, with too many commonplace or impractical ideas and nothing realized or implemented that adds new value. Similarly, an organization that assumes that "innovating" is mysterious, and creativity is solely the preserve of a minority of people who experience a "bolt from the blue", will fail to teach or encourage innovation and so also miss many opportunities.

Lastly, other common mistakes include:

- Dumbing down – calling projects innovative when they aren't devalues the word and wearies employees, draining them of enthusiasm for innovation work;
- New technologies – it is entirely possible to offer new value in a new way, using existing technologies. New technologies can be a gateway to an innovation, but can also become a distraction. The focus of the innovation must always be on providing a new solution to the customer's need in the most appropriate way, which can be a traditional, non-technological way;
- Ignoring incremental or small innovations – there is sometimes an assumption that all innovations must be ground-breaking, and smaller innovations or incremental improvements that could provide increased profits are not sufficiently valued. Not all useful innovations are disruptive. Organizations can get caught up in the hype and waste money searching unnecessarily for a headline innovation, when smaller innovations would be successful; and
- A lack of resources – innovation teams need to be adequately resourced and supported and leaders should ensure that any measurements do not incentivize them to focus on day-to-day work at the expense of innovation work.

Can you measure innovation?

A common area of friction between innovation projects and everyday work is the lack of accountability. Many frontline workers feel that they must deliver quality work under scrutiny, whilst innovation teams may play and fail to deliver (even if failing fast and learning considerable amounts that are useful for the future) without comment. Therefore, it is often a good idea for organizations to investigate the best ways for innovation projects to report in at the highest level.

Innovations are inherently uncertain and simple balance sheet accounting measurements will fail to reflect the learning and development benefits that even unsuccessful innovations bring to the organization.

It can be useful to measure activities and inputs, such as the numbers of suggestions or ideas, or the time spent on innovation projects, but these must be balanced with outputs such as how many new products or services have been released in the past few years, as a proportion of the products/services that your organization offers or the profits/market share that it makes, or customer attitudes towards products and services and their satisfaction with old and new versions. Depending on your organization, you may find that it is more effective to report on milestones for specific innovation projects that focus on learning and knowledge sharing and measure how well the organization is managing the process of innovation, rather than the inputs or outputs.

Next steps – what can you do now?

Having explored in more depth the definitions and process for innovation, your organization's next steps should already be clearer. If you are seeking ways to begin to formalize innovation, consider starting with the following:

- Conduct an analysis of the trends in the market environment, your existing customers' wants and needs, and horizon scan for future potential changes (think "crystal ball" rather than "wide angled lens" or "microscope");
- Consult with customers and employees for ideas on improving processes, products, and services, both internally and externally. Connect with customers for open-minded conversations. Try not to make assumptions about who your customers are and what they want (which often happens when relying on closed question surveys, rather than open conversations) and try to unearth their unarticulated needs. If it helps, create a map of the customer's journey towards fulfilling its needs (think about the hammer/picture hanging example) and see if there are other ways to meet their needs along that journey; and
- Even if you can't afford to gather a diverse innovation team, teach all your employees about the nature and process of innovation (see box). Encourage them to think innovatively and suggest

ideas and changes. Be open to new ideas from unlikely sources. Your organization may already have creative entrepreneurial employees who can be of great value. Use all available resources such as business advisors, grants, and outside assistance. Many universities want to partner with businesses, so investigate local and international collaboration and research opportunities.

Can anyone be innovative? Can we teach innovation?

The innovative ability is within all of us to some degree or another. From childhood we learn naturally by experimentation, learning improved ways of being and doing, whether that is drinking from a cup, learning to spell, or working out which tactics play to our natural abilities to win at sports.

Individuals tend to have a natural preference for creativity or detail/completion at work, but, as with all preferences, individuals can learn the skills necessary for both. In any event, for innovations to be successful, organizations need both creative people and those who ensure that ideas will be realized.

It can be helpful to teach employees generally about innovation, particularly case studies and research that demonstrate successful innovative processes. It can be particularly useful to teach employees creative problem solving and challenging questioning techniques and to give leaders the skills to nurture the cultural elements necessary to support innovation and to act as a bridge between those in different aspects of the business.

For innovative solutions to emerge, it can be useful for teams to spend time on divergent problem solving, when many ideas are collected but not evaluated or judged, then a convergent phase when the many ideas are considered and both nurtured and advanced as well as winnowed down. For employees to use these techniques, it can be useful for them to be taught about the research and thinking behind this.

Although consultants and lecturers can teach what has been learnt so far about successful innovators, in the end, mastering the technique is up to individuals and organizations. Primarily, they need to develop the ability to manage innovations by being humble, curious, and brave. They need to be willing to admit deficiencies and limitations in existing products and services and be prepared to work at understanding value from the customer's or user's point of view, in order to deliver better value in the future, and they need to be open to failure and looking foolish through investigating many different ideas.

Conclusion

In order to realize innovation, organizations must leverage the diversity of their employees, create the right culture for creative problem solving and idea development, and ensure that these are aligned to strategic goals. To facilitate this, leaders must learn to be open-minded and collaborative, comfortable with uncertainty, and able to foster a culture that accepts challenge and change.

Further reading and information

Davenport, T. and Prusak, L., *Working Knowledge*, Harvard Business Publishing Education.
Gardner, H., *Smart Collaboration*, Harvard Business Review Press.
Kim, W. and Mauborgne, R., *Blue Ocean Strategy*, Harvard Business Review Press.
Leonard, D. et al, *Critical Knowledge Transfer*, Harvard Business Review Press.
Leonard-Barton, D. and Swap W., *Making Sparks Fly*, Harvard Business Review Press.
Leonard-Barton, D., *Wellsprings of Knowledge*, Harvard Business Review Press.
Sheffield, R., *How leaders learn to boost creativity in teams: Innovation catalysts*, World Scientific Europe.
Various, *Harvard Business Review on Knowledge Management*, Harvard Business Publishing Education.
Various, *HBR's 10 Must Reads on Innovation*, Harvard Business Publishing Education.
Various, *Innovations in Legal KM*, ed. Lawrence, H., ARK Group.
ISO 30401:2018(E) International Standard for Knowledge Management.
"How to manage for collective creativity," Linda Hill, Professor of Business Administration at Harvard Business School, speaking at TEDx; www.youtube.com/watch?v=ImmtTHYU5GQ

Chapter 2:
Where does innovation sit? Distributed practice innovation at Stewart McKelvey

By Cyndi Murphy, knowledge manager, Stewart McKelvey

In the past, when knowledge management initiatives revolved around the gathering and organization of internal precedents, or the implementation of specific technology, such as a SharePoint portal or enterprise search, the knowledge manager or the knowledge management department had focused control over the success of the initiative. In today's legal market, law firms are leveraging practice innovation to ensure competitive advantage, financial stability, and lawyer retention. Successful initiatives are not the result of work by just one person or one department; success or failure depends on the engagement of multiple individuals and departments.

There are good reasons why successful knowledge management initiatives now – and in the future – will depend on practice innovation driven by multiple departments and individuals. Not every law firm has dedicated knowledge management lawyers or staff. Although technology plays a key role in many practice innovation solutions, by automating routine, repetitive tasks, analyzing large amounts of data, or enabling intuitive user interfaces, knowledge managers have learned through experience that the implementation of the technology is only part of a practice innovation solution. It cannot be a stand-alone project of the IT department, although that expertise is integral. The most important factor for success is the active engagement of lawyers in practice. They need to want to change, to innovate. In order for lawyers to embrace innovation and create profitable productivity in their practice, they need to be engaged and involved in identifying the inefficiencies, frustrations, or roadblocks that prevent them from providing clients with great service; in proposing solutions to the problems they encounter; and in implementing the innovative changes that will provide new areas for growth and maximize profitability.

Proactive knowledge managers recognize this paradigm shift and position themselves to be the facilitators of practice innovation, sharpening their skills in enabling, teaching, coaching, and group dynamics to identify problems and propose solutions, and in change management to implement sustainable innovation.

Stewart McKelvey, a six-office, regional firm in Atlantic Canada, has recognized the need for practice innovation to be embraced, implemented, and shared across the organization. Lawyers, individually and in teams, are involved in identifying, implementing, and sustaining practice innovation initiatives. Multiple departments are involved in facilitating the implementation. Specific staff members are embedded in practice innovation projects.

Practice re-engineering teams

Following an in-depth look at the firm's practice areas, a subcommittee of the partnership board made extensive recommendations on what needed to be done to ensure profitability into the future. Those recommendations included the appointment of a practice innovation partner, the establishment of a practice innovation department, and the creation of practice re-engineering teams.

Recognizing that he would be most effective as the facilitator, rather than the implementer, of any innovative changes made by the re-engineering teams, the practice innovation partner structured the teams for engagement and action. Each team had at least one practice engineer, an associate lawyer whose work on re-engineering projects was compensated, based on time spent and results achieved. Each team also had at least one practice owner, a partner who would oversee the project, champion it, and provide guidance to the engineer. The partner's contributions to the project were also taken into consideration at compensation time. Most of the teams were involved in practice areas that spanned multiple offices, so there was an engineer and owner from each office. The practice innovation partner took responsibility for creating the teams. (There was an initial call for volunteers, but as lawyers subsequently left the practice or found the time commitment unsustainable, he relied on recommendations and personal contact.) He also organized and chaired the regular team "coaching" meetings, and maintained the work plan status of key project deliverables, responsibilities, and timelines that each team developed under his guidance.

The teams now cover diverse practice areas, in both advocacy and business – litigation support; residential real estate; mergers and acquisitions; corporate reorganization; estates and trusts; labor and employment; builders' liens; immigration; insurance defense; and commercial lending.

Each team has developed its own charter in which it states the business case and identifies measurable goals and initiatives. The outcomes are as diverse as the practice areas and reflect the priorities determined by the team members and the lawyers practicing in that area. Examples of re-engineering projects include:

- Creating standard form agreements using document assembly software;
- Championing the subscription to third party databases such as Practical Law Canada and Blue J Legal to supplement and improve internal precedents, checklists, and standard forms;
- Developing flat fee pricing models for specific transactions;
- Leveraging pdf software to standardize and expedite the production of litigation documents;
- Automating for efficiencies the production of documents in a commercial transaction;
- Creating jurisdictional guides to common issues in insurance defense work;
- Supervising the internal development of apps that consolidate matter information, improving the service to the client and making multi-lawyer teams more efficient; and
- Offering training on the practice innovation initiatives implemented by the team.

Most of the teams have been working on practice innovation initiatives for several years now. Completion of one project leads to a spin off project, such as an enhancement or a billing model. In addition to identifying the initiatives on which to work, because team members are on the practice frontlines daily, the lawyers also become the champions for innovation, promoting the use of the new tool or database to the colleagues with whom they are working.

Practice toolbox

Practice toolbox is the area on SmartNet (the Stewart McKelvey SharePoint portal) where practice-related documents and links – checklists, precedents (including internally developed document assembly precedents), samples, guides, process maps, articles, and other useful information – are stored. All of the material is organized using a classification scheme that corresponds, at the highest level, to the matter types assigned to client files. The Handshake software used for SMartNet's user interface enables a user to choose specific areas of practice to display by default.

The Handshake interface also provides the ability for a lawyer to upload useful documents or links to Practice toolbox by clicking on the relevant icon.

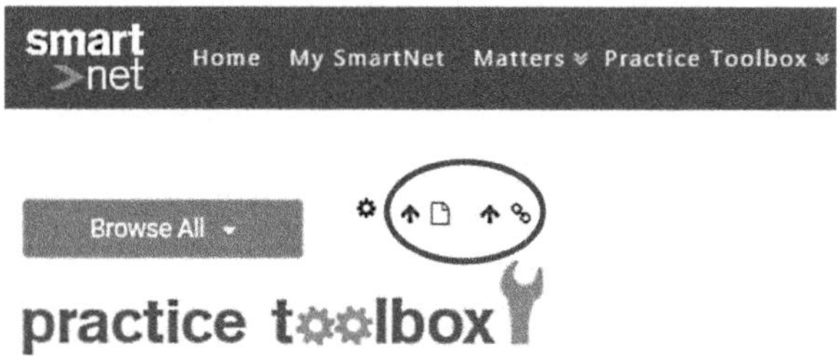

Figure 1: Practice toolbox.

When uploading a document or a link, the lawyer is prompted for additional information – [a descriptive] title, [a detailed] summary, jurisdiction (if applicable), and practice topic (chosen from the classification scheme). If the lawyer does not consider any of the existing practice topics to be relevant, there is an option to suggest a topic.

Any document or link submitted through the icon on the Practice toolbox page goes into a submissions library in SharePoint and the knowledge managers get a notification that there is a submission that requires editing. One of the knowledge managers reviews the submitted record to ensure that all of the fields have been completed and that the practice topic chosen is correct. If there is no practice topic given, one will be assigned, or if a topic is suggested and there is agreement, the knowledge manager will add the topic to the classification. Once the review is complete, and all the fields are filled, the knowledge manager moves the record into the Practice toolbox SharePoint library and deletes the submission.

Only documents or links submitted by lawyers are added to Practice toolbox, i.e., there is no effort by the knowledge managers to search the document management system or other internal resources to locate additional materials. Recently, a field for the practice re-engineering category has been added to the submission template. This enables practice engineers to submit the document assembly precedents their practice re-engineering teams have created using Doxsera. A lawyer can also filter for the re-engineering precedents from the top tab in the Practice toolbox.

Figure 2: Uploading a document.

The upload icons in Practice toolbox make it easy for lawyers to contribute content, and the authors of the shared precedents not only have information they find useful in one place, they get recognized for their contributions.

Health law expert locator

Stewart McKelvey has an active insurance defense practice, as well as a health law practice involved in the malpractice defense of doctors and hospitals. The lawyers in those practices frequently rely on experts' reports and testimony when preparing their advice to clients. Although there had been past attempts to maintain an internal database of experts, the database was outdated and did not contain current information on the health law experts being used by Stewart McKelvey lawyers. The database was being maintained by staff in the library and knowledge services department who were relying on lawyers to provide them with information to be entered; because lawyers did not remember to forward information about additions, deletions, or updates to the database, it was not current.

In identifying the need for a current database, or locator, the lawyers also identified the need for a listing that they could easily use and update themselves. Applying the Lean Six Sigma principle of a minimally viable product, a technician in the practice innovation department created a simple SharePoint list on a team site of the internal portal, SMartNet. It was based on an experts locator previously created by the practice innovation partner. The list included columns for names of the experts, area of expertise, mailing address, telephone number, and email contact. Lawyers in the practice area, and their legal assistants, were given access to the site. Permissions on the site include the ability to upload information directly to the list and edit existing entries.

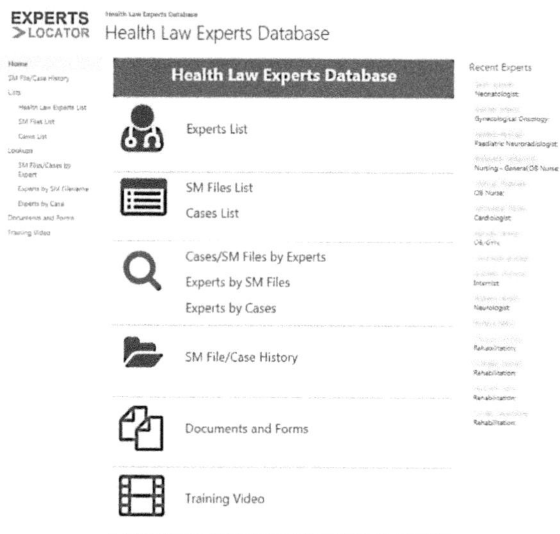

Figure 3: Health law expert locator.

Although the locator was originally designed as a listing of experts, over time the practicing lawyers identified the need for additional functionality. The listing now includes information on reported cases, as well as Stewart McKelvey matters in which the expert has testified. In addition to a full citation, there are hypertext links to the full text of the decision, and details on whether the expert provided evidence for the plaintiff or the defendant, or filed a report. There are also fields for a statement of issues in the case and how the court treated the evidence. A lawyer can also locate a listing by case or matter and obtain information on all of the experts involved. Because the health law expert locator resides on a team site, it is not constrained by the content management protocols and user interface of the main portal.

The currency – and the value of the information in the expert locator – is now dependent on the lawyers themselves. It addresses their needs, and they know the need to address its currency. The value of the locator is enhanced when the lawyers enter comments on their experience with the expert, adding notes on the expert's response to deadlines, ability to explain technical terms clearly, or comportment in court.

DMS implementation

In the fall of 2018, Stewart McKelvey moved from a user-centric document management system to NetDocuments, a matter-centric DMS. Although the firm's matters had been centralized in the accounting system for over a decade, the documents created on those matters resided on separate servers in individual offices. The firm had six different document libraries and each document library had its own list of document types, cumulating in a list of over 1,300 document types. (Stewart McKelvey has six offices in each of the four Atlantic provinces.) Because everyone in the firm would be accessing the documents in a single location after the DMS switch, it was decided, based on the experience of other firms, that Stewart McKelvey would do this as a "big bang". Users left their computers connected to the network on Friday at 5pm when they left for the day. They returned Monday morning at 9am to start saving, and searching for, documents using NetDocuments. There was extensive preparation needed to make that a success and the IT director oversaw many moving parts. This was a major IT project, but the successful transition involved the IT, library and knowledge services, and technology training departments, as well as the manager of change support and training and the practice innovation partner. It also involved lawyers, legal assistants, and paralegals in focus groups to discuss and provide feedback on the proposed new document types.

Before the firm could have its NetDocuments "big bang", it needed to reconcile the 1,300+ document types that were being used throughout the six offices. Only 20 percent of the document types were used 80 percent of the time and some document types had been used only once or twice. No one had responsibility for overseeing the document types, so if IT got a request to create a new one, they did so. As a result of a statistical analysis of the types used most heavily and feedback from focus groups held with lawyers, legal assistants, and administrative staff in all offices, the practice innovation advisory committee (PIAC) approved a final list of 50 new document types compiled by the knowledge manager. PIAC, an advisory group of lawyers who work closely with the practice innovation partner and the chief executive officer, control the addition of any future document types. The matter type is one of the ways in which a user can limit a search in NetDocuments and there are practice group workspaces that correspond to the matter types for precedents, presentations, and other documents that are not client-specific, but need to be shared with others (but are not designated to be added to Practice toolbox). Because of the knowledge management lead on the rationalization of document types, a knowledge manager also participated in regular meetings with the IT director, the manager of change support and training, and the technology trainers to discuss strategies around the introduction of NetDocuments and user training.

The approach to this project minimized the disruption to practice support and client service during the initial phase of NetDocuments use. Users were aware of the changes (and the need for a change of DMS), there were multiple methods of support for the change, and there was opportunity for engagement and feedback before the change took place.

Conclusion

Recently, the CEO of Stewart McKelvey was named one of Atlantic Canada's top 50 chief executive officers for the second year in a row. Nominees for this award, from all industries, were judged, among other criteria, according to their company's growth in recent years. Her leadership and championship of practice innovation contributed to this honor and recognition as practice innovation fuels the firm's growth.

This case study illustrates that a law firm does not need a lot of staff to successfully implement practice innovation initiatives. At Stewart McKelvey, the practice innovation department consists of the practice innovation partner; a manager with experience in software programming; and two technicians, one a previous legal assistant and one trained as a programmer. Staff in the library and knowledge services department, consisting of two knowledge managers, a legal information specialist, a senior library technician, and a part-time filing clerk have content management responsibilities for the SharePoint portal and the research-focused internal databases, but their daily responsibilities are focused on library collection maintenance and reference and research assistance. Other administrative departments, such as IT, are involved in practice innovation when their expertise is required. Stewart McKelvey's success in practice innovation is based on the active involvement of many practicing lawyers, and the leveraging of internal expertise on a project-by-project basis.

Chapter 3: The changing role of the knowledge manager

By Raymond Olayinka, senior advisory consultant, Arup

As the field of knowledge management is evolving, so is the role of the knowledge manager. How will the role change to reflect wider field transformation? What new capabilities will knowledge managers need to develop to keep adding value within organizations and beyond?

Before computers, there were typists...

Before computers, there were professional typists who took shorthand or dictation and typed it up in triplicate. After computers came on to the scene, typists moved from the typing or secretarial pool to the word processing department. Today there are few word processor jobs out there, possibly in law firms, publishing, and government offices. Although the typist profession seems to be disappearing, typing itself has not gone away, and has become more widespread than ever before. The specialist skill that used to be someone's day job is now a capability that is part of everyone's role. Most people in organizations now type their own reports intuitively regardless of their hierarchy or job role. Technology has undoubtedly contributed to the shifting landscape of the typing industry. Now enter the world of voice-to-text technology and it's a different ballgame entirely in which typing may even disappear altogether.

Although the typing profession may not be perfectly analogous to the evolving field of knowledge management (KM), it is worth considering how the field is transforming and how this will affect the role of the knowledge manager. What new capabilities will knowledge managers need to develop to keep adding value within organizations and beyond? It is important to consider three of the viewpoints that have emerged in the past few years from KM authors and commentators: first is that KM is dead and therefore requires no knowledge manager roles; second is that KM is *not* dead but is on life support; third is that KM is alive and will keep thriving in the foreseeable future. Another aspect worth considering is whether KM in organizations will continue as a function with designated job roles, or as a capability in which KM is part of everyone's day job, from the youngest employee to the most senior. Will technology continue to be an enabler of KM, or a disruptor? These will all be discussed in this chapter.

How is knowledge management evolving?

Much has happened in the world of KM and much has been written about it. Whilst not attempting to repeat age-old KM concepts, it is worth contextualizing the topic on the changing role of the knowledge manager. KM has been around for centuries and the quest for understanding knowledge has always been central to human behavior. It came into prominence as a discipline in the early 1990s, driven by the need to capture, store, and distribute knowledge more effectively within organizations, particularly the experiential knowledge of people. This period coincided with internet growth, globalization, and amalgamation of geographically dispersed businesses. Each new advance in communication and learning technology expanded the possibilities for knowledge capture and distribution. Large management consultancies became early adopters of KM and showcased the successes of their own internal KM programs. Some large companies created formal KM posts such as chief knowledge officers (the CKO), introduced new knowledge initiatives, and brought several existing programs under a KM department. By the mid-2000s, the uptake of KM had become widespread across many organizations globally. It was also recognized as a distinct academic discipline, with papers published in KM journals and conferences held across the globe. As web-based and content management technology became more mature, IT-enabled KM solutions became more commonplace. Today, there is a lot of buzz around the ideas of digital workplace and digital transformation, with new tools being acquired by organizations, sometimes without a strong business case. Unfortunately, KM is still mistaken for information management, data management, or document management and this is reflected in the way organizations acquire IT tools in place of an effective KM program. In the foreseeable future, improvements will continue to be made in cognitive computing and artificial intelligence, which are already being used to automate certain KM tasks and augment knowledge-related decision-making. There is increased attention given to analytics, business intelligence, and data science, which help KM use data to derive insights and inform actions and decisions. It will be interesting to see how the latest developments in technology, software, and gadgetry impact KM and knowledge manager roles.

No one sets out to be a knowledge manager...

Have you ever heard anyone say, "When I grow up, I'll like to be a knowledge manager"? Perhaps no one sets out from inception to become a knowledge manager, it just so happens. Most people who hold KM roles today either found themselves in the role or had it thrusted upon them due to a KM need in the organization. Not trying to generalize here; of course there are academics and industry practitioners who set out to research KM and have made immense contributions to the body of knowledge in this field. The knowledge manager role in this context refers to those involved in implementing KM at any level, from strategic to tactical, in organizations. They come from various professional backgrounds such as law, engineering, business, finance, sciences, and arts, from both private and public sectors. Whilst some do KM as an add-on to their day jobs, others do it as a paid full-time role. There are also outward-facing KM consultants who provide advisory services to address clients' KM needs. Most newly appointed knowledge managers in organizations have had to learn about KM on-the-job and figure it out for themselves through reading KM publications, attending KM conferences, learning from case studies from early-adopter organizations and networking with people in the field.

Newbies to KM are initially faced with the challenge of making sense of KM – what it is exactly, and how to define it. Understandably, because there exist myriads of definitions of KM out there that can sometimes appear confusing, conflicting, and overlapping. What is even more daunting is the lack of common terminology and an inconsistent approach to KM processes. Knowledge managers struggle to understand the remit of their roles, let alone explain it to colleagues. It is often said that if you asked ten KM experts to define KM, they would come up with at least 12 different definitions. But beyond the complexities of KM conceptualizations lie the need for knowledge managers to fully comprehend the challenges facing their organizations. For instance, if the challenge of an organization is about geographical dispersion and silo working, KM should be defined along the lines of integrated collaborative working. If the challenge is about loss of knowledge due to high staff turnover, KM should be defined along the lines of preserving the corporate body of knowledge. The challenge also determines the type of

KM roles required to implement KM. In some large organizations, KM is treated as a function with a department headed by a CKO or the head of KM. Other organizations handle KM in a less hierarchical way.

Examples of KM challenges faced	Examples of KM roles required
Innovation, invention, creativity, generation of new knowledge, intellectual property	Knowledge and innovation manager, intellectual capital manager, head of knowledge and intellectual property
Knowledge transfer	Knowledge transfer manager, Knowledge exchange manager, knowledge transfer associate
Fostering collaboration and communities. Enterprise Social Networks (ESN), skills networks, forums, professional practices	Practice leader, skills network leader, forum leader, community leader
Lessons learned, learning from experience (LfE) and knowledge capture and re-use. Learning and competency development	Lessons learned facilitator, LfE hub manager, competency manager
Expert and expertise location, personal profiles	Capability lead, knowledge administrator
Search, findability, taxonomy, metadata, tagging, portals, intranets, and websites. Preserving knowledge assets, corporate body of knowledge	Content manager, knowledge curator, content developer, helpdesk manager, knowledge architect, knowledge asset manager
Analytics, business intelligence, customer/competitor knowledge sharing	CRM manager, knowledge and insight manager, knowledge analyst

Table 1: Examples of KM challenges and KM roles including the CKO.

Good old "People, Process, Technology"

The term "people, process, technology" is no longer a fresh concept but is still useful in explaining the critical success factors for initiatives such as organizational change, business process improvement, transformation programs, IT service management, and knowledge management, and has been integral to the delivery model of such initiatives. Focusing on its application to KM, technology is only as good as the processes that wrap around it, while the processes are only as good as the people that use them. As mentioned earlier, there is no consistency in which the KM process is being portrayed or applied. Some say that you need to first "capture" knowledge, then "store" knowledge, then "diffuse" knowledge in a three-step process. Some say that you need to first "acquire", then "store", "use", and "curate" knowledge in a four-step process and so on. In fact, over the years authors have come up with no less than 50 KM processes (see table 2). Whether these emerged out of passion for the subject or an eagerness to contribute to the body of knowledge, it doesn't make the job any easier.

Identify	Organize	Access	Mobilize	Curate
Source	Transform	Retrieve	Connect	Gather
Select	Compile	Exploit	Learn	Refine
Discover	Coordinate	Disseminate	Use	Inquire
Capture	Structure	Share	Re-use	Synthesize
Acquire	Develop	Transfer	Apply	Improve
Absorb	Filter	Distribute	Leverage	Dispose
Abstract	Store	Sell	Utilize	Transform
Codify	Maintain	Deploy	Create	Assess
Modify	Secure	Diffuse	Generate	Validate

Table 2: Knowledge management processes.

Technology is increasingly becoming the point of focus for KM, rather than a supporting tool. Organizations spend time and resources purchasing fancy IT gadgets, data, and document management tools, often driven by what competitors are buying. Not surprisingly, KM is often mistaken for IT and is treated as such. Successful KM implementation involves acquiring the right technology at the right time for the right purpose. For example, the use of collaboration tools has allowed organizations to mitigate some of the historical KM challenges, such as the difficulty in capturing and transferring tacit knowledge – the knowledge locked in the brains of the experts. Technology has helped to connect people to people, and people to the corporate body of knowledge. Part of the remit of knowledge managers therefore is to set direction for which technology add the most value to KM and offers the most return on investment.

What lies ahead for the knowledge manager?

There are speculations and viewpoints regarding the future of KM. Some say that KM is dead in the sense that it has reached its maturity and has gone past its expiration date. This perhaps stems from the notion that KM job adverts are on the decline; that Google Trends suggests that "knowledge management" is a term rarely searched for anymore; that the post of the CKO is now a rarity; that technology has taken over people; that KM is yesterday's news and people are tired of it. Another viewpoint is that KM is not dead but on life support and in the midst of a sort of identity crisis; that the expertise on KM has become diffused and some good practices introduced several years ago have slipped into oblivion. Others believe that KM is alive and well; that KM is now well established and widely practiced; that there is a better understanding of the real issues that concern KM and organizations.

Considering these three viewpoints, one can easily conclude that KM cannot possibly be dead, and is definitely not on life support. This is a personal opinion, not an attempt to trivialize or discredit other viewpoints. The perception that KM adverts and search are declining may be due to the fact that KM is re-branding and job roles are evolving (see examples of job roles in table 1) but the function of KM remains the same. An advert for a "content manager" is still a function of KM. Although the post of CKO appears to be a rarity, many organizations have identifiable and effective knowledge managers, knowledge networks, knowledge portals, communities of practice and so on. The impact of KM in organizations (private and public sector) continues to be showcased at KM conferences globally and published in KM journals.

So, has KM reached its maturity? Not at all; in fact KM still has a very long way to go. Much effort has been focused on managing knowledge at personal and organizational levels but there is still a lot to be done with project and industry level knowledge (see table 3).

Knowledge level	Description
Personal knowledge	Individual knowledge. Experiential. Tacit. Expertise. Historical.
Organizational knowledge	Collective knowledge. Corporate memory. Specialisms. Knowledge domain
Project knowledge	Collaborative knowledge generated by two or more organizations e.g. joint venture projects, supply chain partnerships
Industry/global knowledge	Knowledge transfer within and across industry. Global knowledge sharing

Table 3: Knowledge levels.

When two or more organizations come together to work on a project, they generate a lot of knowledge. How is the knowledge captured? Where should the knowledge be stored? How can this knowledge be accessed and made available when needed? Who owns the intellectual property? Organizations are now pushing to develop lessons learned hubs, legacy learning portals, wikis, and so on where content can be stored in various formats accessible to those who need it. At industry and global level, there is a critical need to systematically and efficiently develop, organize, share, and integrate knowledge to achieve cross-cutting goals. This affects almost every sector, including the nuclear industry, oil and gas, infrastructure, and manufacturing. Intergovernmental organizations require strategies for knowledge transfer, capacity building, and using evidence and lessons from a global and country perspective. These are just a few of the challenges that lie ahead for the knowledge manager.

What new capabilities will knowledge managers need to develop?

Knowledge managers at strategic level need to know the "what, why, how and who" of KM; in other words, they need a good understanding of the KM background and context. Although some of the skills required for KM are generic management skills, an effective knowledge manager needs more in-depth understanding of KM theory and concepts before attempting to implement it. They need to get a grasp of ISO 30401:2018, which sets requirements and provides guidelines for establishing, implementing, maintaining, reviewing, and improving an effective management system for knowledge management in organizations. Knowledge managers should be able to develop and deploy KM strategy, policy, and an implementation plan. Capabilities can be split into technology-related skills and non-technology related skills (see table 4).

Technology related	Non-technology related
Knowledge hub development, enterprise social networks, digital workspace, enterprise search, data science, cognitive computing, machine learning, AI, chatbots, collaborative team spaces, working out loud, gamification, automation etc.	KM maturity assessment, knowledge risk assessments, knowledge health checks, knowledge retention and transfer, communities of practice facilitation, knowledge domain mapping, capability management, skills matrix, storytelling, culture and behaviors.

Table 4: Examples of KM capabilities.

There is a thin line between IT and KM, and knowledge managers should be mindful therefore not to veer too much into IT territory or get bogged down in back-end solutions development, except by choice. In the case of AI, machine learning, blockchain, cognitive computing, coding, automation, data science and so on, knowledge managers need to have at least a basic understanding of these tools and how they fit into the big picture of KM. In reality, employees (end-users) want a great intranet, a great search engine, a great wiki, a great media library, a great document management system, a great virtual collaborative workspace, and a great expert and expertise locator. The role of the knowledge manager is to facilitate the development of these tools, to support end-users in capturing requirements, to interface with the IT department in developing the best solutions, to separate fad from useful tools, and to recommend the most viable tools. The truth is that most employees just want the most user-friendly IT systems to do their day jobs; they don't want systems that are difficult to use, that become a job in itself.

Perhaps the most important capability for the knowledge manager is human relations and stakeholder management. KM is firstly a "people business" before process and technology; therefore the knowledge manager should be able to conduct stakeholder analysis and understand levels of power, influence, interest, and support. Many KM programs have failed due to poor stakeholder management and the inability to carry people along on the journey, thereby damaging the KM brand. The knowledge manager needs the skills to be able to mobilize an "army" of supporters – call them KM champions, KM agents, KM evangelists, KM coordinators, or KM working groups embedded in various departments across the organization. Knowledge managers will need a combination of hard skills and soft skills to implement KM. Hard skills include the use of a range of tools while soft skills include facilitation, building relationships, networks, and communities.

On a concluding note...

If a specialist function like typing can evolve into a commonplace capability, perhaps KM can too, but not in the foreseeable future it seems. Ideally, KM in organizations should be everybody's job and embedded within management systems. However, the old saying that "everybody's job is nobody's job" currently applies to KM, even though the industry is evolving, and the use of technology is becoming widespread. KM is still a function and needs roles, responsibilities, and an implementation program, at least until it becomes second nature and part of the organizational culture. Although technology is increasingly becoming the point of focus for KM, it remains an enabler and supporting tool, not a disruptor. Successful KM implementation involves acquiring the right technology at the right time for the right purpose, not as a result of fad. Contrary to the views that KM is dying or on life support, it is actually thriving and will continue to do so. KM may have reached saturation in theory and concepts but has not reached maturity in practice. Much effort has been focused on managing knowledge at personal and organizational levels but KM has to progress beyond organizations into projects, industry, and global knowledge capture, retention, and transfer. This create opportunities for knowledge managers to work in KM advisory roles, delivering multi-sector and multi-national work. The knowledge manager role requires a combination of hard skills and soft skills. Hard skills include the use of a range of KM tools, while soft skills include facilitation, building relationships, networks, and communities. Surely, the KM environment is evolving with technology advances such as cognitive computing, AI, machine learning, data science gamification, among other "buzzwords". Knowledge managers need to be aware of these tools and how they fit into the big picture of KM. Regardless of technology advances, there will always be the human side of KM, and as long there are humans, knowledge managers will have a role to play.

Chapter 4: Facilitating collaboration

By Sara Traynor, Sara Traynor Consulting

How does your organization cultivate collaboration? Are there targeted outcomes as a result of a strategic approach or is collaboration just left to happen organically? If your aim is to create enduring innovation, facilitating department-wide and organization-wide collaboration is key.

This chapter outlines three established tools for facilitating collaboration:

1. River project – an in-depth process of sharing knowledge and innovations;
2. LEGO® Serious Play® – a facilitated framework for enhancing collaboration by increasing psychological safety to enhance communication, thinking, and problem solving; and
3. Random coffees – a simple scheme demonstrating the value of a chance "water-cooler" chat.

Each of the above is demonstrated using a case study outlining method, outcomes, and lessons learned when applied at Stephens Scown LLP, an employee-owned, mid-sized law firm, along with other organizations looking to develop innovative business practices.

An honest assessment of each tool provides overarching process guidance, as well as learning points for future implementation. The intention is to give a candid window into the process of applying each tool, with the hope that this will enable readers to find a more direct route to success.

Although it wasn't all plain sailing, all three tools were vastly beneficial. Not only did collaboration increase within teams, but departments that were previously distant began working together in entirely unexpected ways.

You don't need to be a coach or workshop facilitator to know that tools are best selected based on the need at hand. My hope is that this chapter helps you to see which interventions may be best for your organization, if it is committed to encouraging innovation through collaboration.

Case study 1: The river project – collaborating on knowledge

If you bought an apple pie from a particular supermarket anywhere in the country, it would be identical, whether you had visited the supermarket in Birmingham, Glasgow, or Southampton. If you went to a law firm and asked for a lease, would it be identical regardless of which office of the firm you had walked into? Sticking with the baked goods metaphor, what if Bristol's pie had a crumble topping, Taunton's a lattice pastry, and London's solid pastry? Is that fair to you as a client – or efficient for the firm? Are there inefficiencies in the processes or gaps in knowledge to address?

Of course, each of the apple pies would be delicious, and all the leases of high quality, with excellent client service, but are they coming at the cost of re-inventing the wheel in each office, each department, or even perhaps within each team? These were the questions posed by Robert Camp in 2016, then the managing partner of a *Sunday Times* 100 Best Companies law firm, with three branches across the south-west.

Robert knew that the firm's lawyers were busy serving clients well, and yet he could also see how multiple members of staff might potentially be trying to solve the same problem as someone in another office or team.

The purpose of the river project was to encourage knowledge sharing among lawyers and support staff both between and within different offices of the same firm. Crucially, the river project looked to streamline the services provided across the firm. The focus was on streamlining "the business of law" – how the teams operated and served clients.

As mentioned in the introduction, let's first look at the methods of this tool, followed by the outcomes, and wrap up with some key lessons learned.

The river project – method

At the core of the river project was the river diagram.

This is a diagnostic tool originally developed by international knowledge management consultant Chris Collison[1] and Geoff Parcell when they were both working at BP plc. Chris led an initial half-day workshop with representatives of each team to create a maturity model. I used this as the basis for the project. The method is detailed in their book, *No More Consultants*.[2]

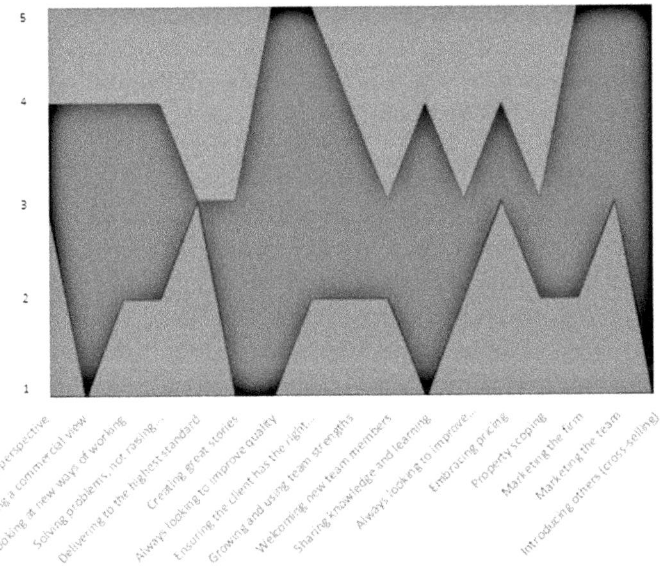

Figure 1: The river diagram.

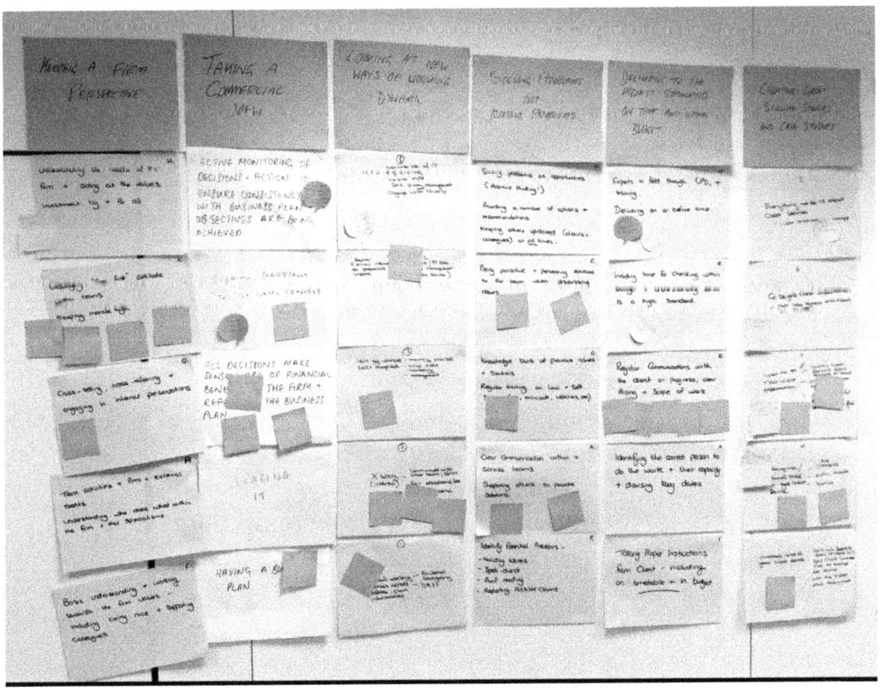

Figure 2: A maturity model.

The first phase of the project was to lead each team in a workshop where they would assess themselves against the maturity model. The model had 17 columns (criteria) and 5 rows (from "1 – adequate" up to "5 – world class"). The criteria the teams would assess themselves against included headings such as Marketing, Pricing, Scoping, Taking a commercial view and Welcoming new team members. Within each square of the model there was a written definition of what behaviors need to be expressed in order to reach that level for each team (e.g. have a written business plan, all team members have read and understand the business plan). The outputs of this workshop were "Offers" and "Requests". Offers were areas where the team was already at levels 4 or 5; they had knowledge to share. Requests were where the team had assessed itself at levels 1 or 2; they would benefit from learning from others who were already at levels 4 or 5.

My role was not to judge or solve a team's issues there and then; it was to help them assess where they were on the model in relation to each of the 17 criteria. This was the first step in a project to foster a collaborative approach to team assessment and then to sharing knowledge and learning from each other.

It is always important for a facilitator to work towards a space of psychological safety. The teams included a variety of roles – lawyers, trainees, and support staff – and it was important for the success of the workshop that all felt listened to. Thankfully, we saw clear evidence that this was achieved, for example when a secretary felt able to challenge an emerging consensus that her team had good internal communication.

She recommended that the assessment for that column be "Adequate", because there were stipulations within the "Good" definition that she didn't feel that the team met. As might be expected, there was a slightly awkward pause. I invited further comments both for and against her point of view, and then offered the suggestion that if one member did not feel that the team's comms was Good, it, by definition, would be difficult for the rest of the team to override her. To the credit of the team, they agreed with her point of view and marked themselves as adequate.

Following the hour-long workshops, I created three outputs:

1. A diagram showing each team's assessment across the 17 criteria;
2. A river diagram, which combined assessments from three teams from each discipline – where the river is widest is where there is the greatest difference in skills and, therefore, where there can be sharing of knowledge; and
3. A written report, describing the river diagram in words.

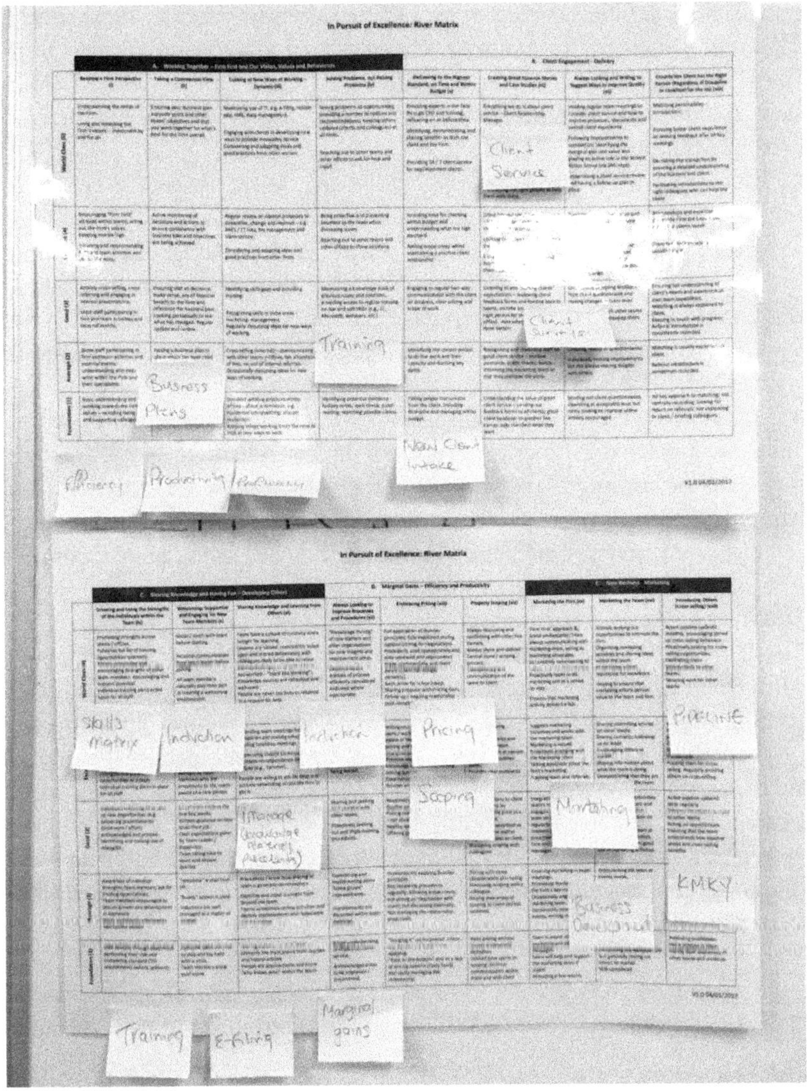

Figure 3: Firm projects mapped on to the maturity model.

Armed with these three resources, I organized meetings with each team's knowledge ambassador and team leader. We discussed some potential areas of growth for their team and how they could use the river diagram to request learning from other teams, as well as offer their own.

Whole team meetings were then held to present results from the workshops and diagrams, with the aim of identifying their top three priority goals. Not only did we discuss which goals they had identified, but we also defined steps that would be taken in order to reach them. This might include, for example, the knowledge ambassador (KA) from the Exeter Family Law team getting in touch with the Truro Family Law KA in order to learn how they might best develop their internal communications.

The whole team meetings concluded the set-up phase of the river project. The following steps kicked off the active phase.

Monthly meetings were set up with the knowledge ambassadors in order to help them project manage their team's movement towards the chosen goals. The meetings also served as an opportunity for the different knowledge ambassadors to share their learning and progress with others. The monthly meetings continued for around 18 months.

The final forum for sharing was a knowledge fair. I tempted everyone along with pizza one lunchtime, and invited each team to showcase their strengths and progress. Not only did this boost morale across offices, but it also led to an unusual but welcome sharing of standard documents.

Let's dive into the outcomes in a bit more detail in the next section.

The river project – outcomes

Though many of the river project's outcomes were intended (increased collaboration, closer working across offices, standardizing certain documents), others were impossible to envision at the beginning of the project.

These by-products were the result of keeping the project flexible. I encouraged the knowledge ambassadors to consolidate any spontaneous benefits that they thought would be useful.

Regardless of whether they were originally intended or not, below are the noticeable outcomes from the river project, along with a few quotes from staff members:

- New materials created – business plans, "month in numbers" infographic reports, staff skills matrices, and many more templates;
- An improvement in relationships between team members (one partner said he'd seen a positive difference in the team just from the initial one-hour workshop);
- A more aligned approach in the business of law across the firm;
- Stronger connections between teams of different disciplines, leading to an increased strength of firm-wide identity:
    - *"I didn't think the Family team could learn anything from the Corporate team!"*

- Closer relationships, so that disciplines felt more like teams across multiple locations:
    - *"Our team were arguably the least connected across offices of all the teams in the firm. Now we have leapfrogged most teams and we are one of the most connected."*
- Recognition that collaborating and standardizing certain documents benefited clients, lawyers, the firm and weren't using their time most efficiently, and how they could combat this in the future through collaborating more closely on projects and materials; and
- Increased ambition to improve – as can be seen from the quotes above, there was some healthy competition and pride!

The above outcomes signaled that the river project was a success. There are, however, a number of lessons learned to consider.

The river project – lessons learned

Thinking right back to the beginning of the river project, one or two people from each team to help decide the text for the maturity model. This inherently created ownership of and enthusiasm around the model, which aided motivation.

Some challenges I worked hard to overcome included the impact of people's pride and the teams' competitiveness. Whilst competitiveness was encouraged, I needed to temper it at times. Occasionally, some teams were disgruntled that others had "scored themselves too highly", making their offers not as valuable. To face these challenges, I provided plenty of reassurance around how the purpose of this exercise was not to score the highest, necessarily, but to have made the largest improvement, and reinforced the fact that this would benefit all involved.

Another difficulty was time constraint, as is natural in a law firm. The 24 team workshops were reduced from Chris' recommended two hours to the single hour. The lesson learned here is that (although more time would have been helpful) with meticulous planning and structured delivery, I was able to facilitate efficient time usage while still gathering enough information to create river diagrams. However, a longer workshop would have allowed for more discussion.

A feature of the river project I would certainly have changed was the number of criteria – 17 was far too many in this instance. The criteria were very broad so there was naturally some cross-over with other projects. Some knowledge ambassadors sensibly decided to combine some together – pricing and scoping, for example.

Other brief takeaways:

- Many lawyers preferred the written reports over the visual river diagrams;
- Engagement really did pay off – the teams that were fully committed benefitted from more of the outcomes;
- Coffee, juice, and fruit helped create a welcoming atmosphere to the team workshops – one team leader, who arrived straight from another meeting, immediately relaxed, exclaiming "Coffee! Great!";
- Teams that were already innovative shared more than they learned – to be expected, and perhaps pre-empted next time around;
- Knowledge ambassadors held a variety of roles in the firm (associate, partner, paralegal, coordinator), which helped to give broad and diverse perspectives, although at times paralegals didn't feel they had the authority to mandate their teams to take action;
- There was unequal distance between some levels – for example, progression from Adequate to Good took much longer than Good to Excellent – and this occasionally impacted motivation; and
- An internal marketing campaign may have helped keep the river project uppermost in everyone's minds between sessions.

The quantity of lessons learned is not to diminish the achievements of the river project. It is critical to reflect – there will always be ways to improve. I also wanted to pass on my learnings to anyone thinking of deploying the river project themselves!

In conclusion, the river project demonstrates that, even in the best companies, knowledge sharing doesn't happen when left to itself. Best practice involves actively pursuing collaboration through innovative interventions. Furthermore, increased internal knowledge sharing reduces a firm's need for external consultant training.

Case study 2: LEGO® Serious Play® – a framework for creating psychological safety

I've already mentioned the phrase psychological safety. But what exactly is it and why is it important?

Professor Amy C. Edmondson,[2] a leading Harvard Business School researcher, states that psychological safety "describes perceptions of the consequences of taking interpersonal risks in a particular context such as a workplace".[3]

Edmondson has identified the importance of psychological safety in the areas of workplace collaboration and teamwork. Psychologically safe team members "feel confident that no one on the team will embarrass or punish anyone else for admitting a mistake, asking a question, or offering a new idea".[4]

Team members who feel psychologically safe are able to be vulnerable and take risks – they're less concerned that others will have a negative reaction to them offering a particular opinion, idea, or perspective.

These benefits lead to better teamwork and innovation and help people see that their work is valued and meaningful. Google was pleased to find Amy Edmonson's work as it explained the findings of its 2012 Project Aristotle. This initiative studied hundreds of Google's teams to figure out why some stumbled while others soared. The soaring teams exhibited behaviors such as equal airtime in discussions. The result was psychological safety, leading to better ideas and outcomes.[5]

LEGO® Serious Play®[6] is a facilitated methodology that encourages psychological safety. This occurs through promoting a number of behaviors and skills, including:

- Equal talking time;
- Increased empathy;
- Space for introverts to think and share; and
- Genuine listening, not just "waiting to speak".

LEGO® Serious Play® – method

LEGO® Serious Play® was originally created in the late 1990s to help the board of the LEGO Group with strategic planning, communication, and creative thinking. They made a creative product (LEGO!) and were frustrated that their strategy wasn't as creative as it could be. Since then it has been used in organizations such as Google, NASA, Coca-Cola, and Unilever.

Although it was designed for a board of, say, 10–12 people, it can also be used for larger and smaller numbers. I have used LEGO® Serious Play® successfully with management teams, with large teams' annual away days, with a small number of board members as well as on a masterclass with a dozen individuals from different organizations.

In this case study I will combine the findings from several LEGO® Serious Play® sessions. The purposes were different and will be useful to list:

- The Devon Air Ambulance Trust's (DAAT) operational management team (OMT) had a mixture of some long-standing employees (up to 22 years) and some people very new to the organization (three to six months). They got on very well as a team but they wanted to accelerate the "sense of team";
- The away days were for two different groups of lawyers – a litigation team of 40 people, and a corporate team of 25 people. Each was made up of three geographical teams based across three offices. The purpose was to work more closely together, regardless of geography, and to agree on their approach to their business plans for the following financial year;
- The board members were new to this board and wanted to understand the agendas and motivations of each other; and
- The purpose of LEGO® Serious Play® at the masterclass was for each individual to consolidate what they had learnt about applying the new KM ISO 30401 standard.

In the away days the morning was spent on LEGO® Serious Play® and the afternoon on a more traditional workshop method. In LEGO Serious Play the facilitator asks a series of questions designed to address the purpose. For each question, everyone builds a model in silence, which represents their answer to the question. Participants only have two to three minutes to do this. Then each person is invited to hold up their model and describe it to the group before answering a series of questions revolving around:

- What each liked about their work;
- What each member brings to the team; and
- Actions each member could take to enable their organization to grow.

The afternoon had a more traditional workshop structure focused on how they would implement their growth ideas to achieve their business plan.

Figure 4: LEGO® Serious Play® workshop model

LEGO® Serious Play® – outcomes

With each of the different groups, from management team to multi-site team to board members, there were consistent outcomes of:

- Insights into each other's perspectives;
- Innovative ideas sparked by deeper thinking and listening; and
- Actions that all members were committed to taking.

Using the LEGO® Serious Play® method created psychological safety. This had instantaneous impacts – team members felt more able to voice their thoughts, as well as more effectively listen to others. Introverts and extroverts shared roughly equal airtime. More ideas were heard and understood. A richer conversation happened.

In the DAAT management team session, one member who had initially expressed concern about "not being creative" ended up building an incredibly intricate model expressing how the organization was being protected from cyber threats. This engaged the imagination of all the team.

Participants gave the following feedback:

"It really made me appreciate my team colleagues as individuals."

"A chance to celebrate our differences."

"[The benefit was understanding] individual OMT members' perspectives."

"[The part of the day I most enjoyed was] Lego as a method for encouraging conversation."

"Good reminder to all that everyone's ideas are valid."

"The use of Lego was creatively fun."

LEGO® Serious Play® – lessons learned

The LEGO® Serious Play® method worked well for all different-sized teams.

For most, the very first question provided eye-opening insight. It only took one question for the board members to discover they had the same ultimate goal. With subsequent builds and guided facilitation they realized they had complementary skills. This propelled and reassured them of their success over the year ahead.

In the afternoon of the away days, without the LEGO® Serious Play® environment, some tables reverted back to a more unequal working environment. One or two voices often dominated the conversation and some people said very little. The dominant voices were usually more senior and often male. To have mitigated this and still achieved equal airtime (without LEGO® Serious Play®) would have required more facilitators than the budget would allow.

Not everyone took to the method. Whilst a couple of people with concerns at the beginning became the most enthusiastic builders, others (maybe two out of over 70 people in total) did not feel it was "serious" enough. This is to be expected and managed so that everyone else experiences the benefits.

In conclusion, the benefits of LEGO® Serious Play® were experienced throughout each session and allowed greater equity in discussions, leading to more innovative ideas and greater buy-in for actions. Professor Amy Edmonson's theory on psychological safety, as well as explaining Google's highest performing teams, is also the secret behind LEGO® Serious Play®.

Case study 3: Random coffees – a simple human-to-human solution

We've all experienced it: mulling over a problem while making a cuppa, making small-talk with a colleague, sharing your thoughts and having them reflect with a unique perspective that gives you that lightbulb moment.

Random coffees is all about creating those inspiring water-cooler moments – random occurrences don't have to be down to chance. Scheduled serendipity may be an oxymoron, but Random coffees counts the NHS, Cabinet Office, BAE Systems, Linklaters and many more large organizations amongst its exponents.

It helps counteract issues that arise due to people rarely having a chance to speak in person to someone who isn't in their team or project. People working in different offices, different floors – or possibly on the desk just around the corner – may not (and most likely will not) share the experiences, skills, perspectives, and knowledge that others have. Work that could be referred internally is less likely to get referred correctly, and may leak out of the organization.

Random coffees – method

In this instance, I ran Random coffees in rounds of three months within a law firm. In month one, people were invited to participate and educated as to the benefits they could gain. I randomly matched people. Months two and three were for the coffees to take place. The scheme comprised of six rounds over two years in spring, summer, and autumn.

The only agenda for the coffee meetings was for participants to get to know each other. It was entirely up to the pair to decide how they used the time – perhaps they discussed their specialisms and common challenges, but they were just as welcome to talk about their home life and family.

Participants completed a short survey after each meeting. The purpose of this was not to scrutinize what they talked about, but to understand what they found beneficial or not about the scheme.

I learned the simple but effective approach of Random Coffees from the NHS.[7] The original idea was developed at Nesta UK, an innovation charity that aims to help people bring ideas to life. At the law firm, the scheme was entirely voluntary and turned out to be very popular.

Random coffees – outcomes

There were a number of benefits to Random coffees. Some depended on the subject of the conversation – for example, those who decided to share non-work topics felt more connected:

> *"Their background, interests, work history, family life etc. all helps to build a picture of who they are and that rapport will benefit us both professionally."*

The small amount of input created great benefits, and led to increased rapport:

> *"Just a quick chat can pay dividends and you should never be too busy to make time for your colleagues."*

> *"Gaining a greater understanding of the experiences and aspirations of a colleague leading to improved relationships in the office."*

There were also professional outcomes, including:

> *"Finding out more about private client and what services they offer their clients."*

> *"Interesting to find out what a trainee thought about the firm and what we were doing that they were impressed with."*

Random coffees – lessons learned

Despite the comparatively "light-touch" method of Random coffees, there were a number of things I noted:

- For future years, avoid a sense of repetition by running the scheme for a shorter period, or on alternate years;
- Different levels of interaction were preferred – some volunteered once, and felt like that was enough for them, whereas others returned time and time again;
- Some people requested specific pairings (which of course contravened the "random" aspect!), showing that the scheme had given permission for people to catch up without a specific business reason;
- When there were a few levels of seniority between the two participants, perceived benefits were sometimes lower; one senior member fed back they had not gained much by having coffee with a secretary. However, there were many instances where partners found it helpful to understand the challenges of support staff, and vice versa; and
- Time and cost input will be questioned, so leadership staff had to be comfortable with benefits that are qualitative rather than quantitative.

In summation, Random coffees was a successful yet low-cost collaborative initiative for the firm.

Benefits were drawn from people sharing common challenges, getting to know each other on a personal level, understanding what each other or their teams do more specifically – and occasionally all three!

Random coffees can easily be run on a spreadsheet by one person in the organization, so if you're thinking about dipping a toe into innovative ways of encouraging organic collaboration, this would be a low-cost low-maintenance initiative to try.

Recommendations for facilitating increased collaboration

In conclusion, there are many effective means of facilitating increased collaboration that can be conducted in an afternoon or over months and years.

Any plans you have to increase collaboration need to be well-planned and structured. The last thing you want a push for collaboration to achieve is pushing teams apart. Indeed, there is a phenomenon known as collaboration overload, whereby performance suffers and burnout risk increases, all as a result of more meetings, requests, emails and phone calls.[8]

Therefore, if you're thinking of facilitating increased collaboration in your organization, begin by articulating answers to the following questions:

- What is the ultimate aim or purpose?
- How will your business know when the goal has been reached?
- What is the scope – organization-wide, focused on one project or team, time and resource budgets?

This should aid you in choosing from the three tools presented. To quickly summarize:

- A river project can create organization-wide alignment in knowledge sharing, via significant time and financial investment over the course of one to two years;
- LEGO® Serious Play® is an innovative way of solving problems innovatively. It is a good option when looking to ensure you create psychological safety to elicit all the ideas in the room (not just the loudest); and

- Random coffees is light touch, low cost, flexible, and with a low resource requirement in terms of initial administration.

Driving innovation, building inter-team and interpersonal relationships, and sharing knowledge will always benefit a business – even if those outcomes are mainly qualitative.

Once you determine how you want collaboration to look, the recommendations in this chapter can help make it a huge success.

References

1. www.chriscollison.com/blog/2010/09/16/km-tools-creating-a-river-diagram
2. *No More Consultants*, Geoff Parcell, Chris Collison, Wiley, 2010.
3. https://web.mit.edu/curhan/www/docs/Articles/15341_Readings/Group_Performance/Edmondson%20Psychological%20safety.pdf
4. www.annualreviews.org/doi/full/10.1146/annurev-orgpsych-031413-091305
5. https://rework.withgoogle.com/guides/understanding-team-effectiveness/steps/identify-dynamics-of-effective-teams/
6. www.nytimes.com/2016/02/28/magazine/what-google-learned-from-its-quest-to-build-the-perfect-team.html
7. www.rasmussenconsulting.dk/
8. www.slideshare.net/HorizonsCIC/how-to-set-up-a-randomised-coffee-trial
9. https://hbr.org/2016/01/collaborative-overload

Chapter 5: Sustaining innovation through managing knowledge

By Dr Randhir Pushpa, founder and chief consultant, ACIES Innovations

Innovation and innovating have a strong linkage with knowledge. Understanding this linkage will help us manage innovation programs much better and lessen the mystery around innovation. Knowledge management as a practice focuses on helping organizations leverage knowledge in a planned manner to achieve business benefits. The role of "managing knowledge" and how it can be leveraged to create a culture of innovation or manage innovation programs needs to be understood properly. This chapter focuses on the role KM interventions play in helping organizations be more innovative.

There are two very common ways organizations practice innovation. The first, which is a more common approach to innovating, starts with an idea or a need. It can be in the form of a product, product feature, process, delivery model, or business model. This need or idea gets crystallized into a specific requirement, which then gets transformed into a solution. The second relates to creating an innovative culture, which mostly focuses on creating thought leadership in any specific area or simply to be known as an innovative organization. Let us analyze both the approaches and understand how both of them rely on knowledge management practices.

From idea/need to innovative solution

In the first case the journey starts from a need or idea, which then gets converted into specific requirements. The need or idea may come from a market survey, understanding of client requirement, from thought leadership thinking or may be a requirement that comes from the leadership team. In many cases the idea or need itself will not be groundbreaking; the implementation is where innovation happens. Note that the level of innovation required in the solution is already defined and the team just needs to achieve that. For example, the idea or need may be something new to the world, industry, or to the organization. The effort the development team needs to put depends on the level of innovativeness of the requirement. This is something very common across most industries.

Let us take the case of the touchscreen feature in Smartphones. Smartphones started becoming popular in the early 2000s, with their ability to provide many more services beyond calling and messaging services provided by feature phones. Of all the features provided in the smartphone, what defined them in the initial days was the touchscreen. Touchscreen is a technology that helps a user interact directly with applications by touching instead of using a mouse or a keyboard. This feature probably nailed it for Apple and established it as a key player in the smartphone market. Touchscreen technology consists of three components – the touch sensors, the controllers that convert voltage charges into signals, and software that helps the signals connect with the application to pass the communication.

The idea of having a touchscreen feature in a mobile phone may have originated in a CEO's mind and the CEO may have asked his team to develop one. Note that the idea may be an incredible one, but innovative behavior is required in the implementation. Once the requirement of creating a touchscreen interface for a smart phone was given, a team was assembled to achieve it, with cost and timeline as key controlling factors along with the requirement. While idea generation is an important part of this innovation, in many cases it is a miniscule part and the actual innovative work happens when the team sits down to make the idea a reality. The IP lies in how to convert the idea into reality. Even when a patent is granted, it is not for the idea, but how the idea gets converted into a solution. What is critical is knowledge.

The process of staffing a team is an activity in ensuring relevant knowledge is available within the team. This process is knowingly or unknowingly done, keeping in mind the different kinds of knowledge that will be required to develop the product. Intelligence and experience of the staffing team comes into play here. If the staffing is done considering the technical skills required rather than the soft skills, the team may find it difficult to manage all the stress that goes with product development. Hence, the staffing team should understand the different kinds of knowledge that will be required to develop solutions and accordingly identify the right team members.

Now let us see how this team would go about developing the solution. Most probably the team would start off by researching whether anyone has already worked on this solution and if possible how they have done it. They will try to get as much information and knowledge as possible about this by referring to journals, industry publications, competitor products and talking to experts. One can see a natural approach towards gathering knowledge on prior art. If there are no support systems created to help the team search relevant knowledge, they will struggle in their attempt. Hence it is important that the innovation team is provided with easy access to knowledge in the form of reference materials and experts. In many cases it is difficult to foresee the different kinds of knowledge a team will require. Even if it may be possible, it may not be economical to have all the knowledge within the team. The best approach will be to create a team with the most relevant knowledge and then help them create a network of experts to reach out to for quick support.

Consider that the team could not come across any references of touchscreens for mobile phones. In other words, they could not find any knowledge of how to make a touchscreen for phones from literature. This would mean there is no know-how of how to create a touchscreen for smartphones. They will have to create new know-how of how to create the solution. They may come out with a conceptual framework and then develop the solution based on that. After many experiments they would create a touchscreen for a smartphone that adheres to the requirements of the CEO.

What has actually happened is that the team starts creating new knowledge of how sensors can be made to recognize touch, how the sensors can convert the touch into signals, and how the application can understand these signals. Each of them is a knowledge generation scenario. Along with the creation of the solution, the team would also have evolved know-how of how to create the solution. The production team will then capture the know-how of how to create the solution by discussion with the product development team and, based on that, manufacture the solution.

If we recap this journey, we can identify the following key areas where KM interventions are done:

- Team staffed, considering the complexity of the idea/need, by ensuring all the relevant knowledge is with the team;
- Knowledge base provided to find knowledge from research and work done by other organizations; and
- Easy access to expert knowledge for knowledge missing within the team.

Creating and sustaining an innovative culture

Now let us consider the scenario where we have to build an innovative culture. This is a much more difficult problem for most organizations, since there is no direction for innovation like the earlier case, but the need is to innovate and create innovative products.

Let's consider a case study about an intervention carried out in the Bangalore office of a multinational company. This company, which is into software products and IT services domains, has offices across the world and works on emerging technologies. The Bangalore office is a captive development center of the R&D division of the company. The objective of the Bangalore center is to work and support the global R&D team, which is spread across Europe and US. The nature of the work is highly complex and the Bangalore center is required to not only scale up but exhibit innovative behavior. When the intervention was done, the Global R&D team's average experience was around 25 years, while the average age of employees in the Bangalore center was around 27 years. There was huge pressure on the team to live up to the high expectations of the global teams and prove that they could work on complex projects.

The Bangalore development center's leadership team realized that they had two challenges. One was to convince the global team that they could manage complex projects and the other was to create a culture where the Bangalore team was comfortable working on complex projects. To do that they came up with an idea of focusing on patenting. They realized that patenting is a good approach to solve both the challenges, since the global R&D team was measured on the number of patents filed and the employees in the Bangalore center had a feeling that generating patentable ideas and filing patents was very difficult, something that only experts are able to do.

The responsibility of promoting an innovation culture and promoting patenting came to the KM team, as it was staffed by a few members who were experienced in managing innovation projects. Since the KM team had exposure to both knowledge management and innovation management, they could see the relevance of managing and leveraging knowledge. Accordingly, they evolved an implementation program that would help in creating patenting culture and as a result improve innovativeness. The different interventions implemented as part of promoting a culture of patenting are shared below.

Facilitating sharing and collaboration

Sharing and collaboration are essentially means of transferring knowledge and bringing together different employees. Employees seek knowledge when they do not have sufficient knowledge to perform a task. A culture of sharing and collaboration makes it easy for employees to find relevant knowledge. However, sharing and collaboration helps in another way in the case of promoting innovation. It helps employees get in touch with others who have significantly different types of knowledge. Since innovation mostly happens when diverse knowledge comes together, a sharing and collaboration culture is very important, breaking down silos and making it easy for employees from various groups to come together and discuss comfortably. For the Bangalore center employees, the culture of sharing and collaboration was enabled through online and offline sharing sessions and workshops. Enterprise social networking platforms were extensively used to promote better communication. Online platforms can also help in creating special interest groups, where likeminded employees can come together, share ideas, discuss challenges or evolve new ideas.

Equipping with relevant knowledge

Sharing and collaboration has enabled faster transfer of knowledge between diverse people. However, it is important that employees are properly skilled and have access to learning materials. The learning and development team focused on skilling employees with relevant knowledge, based on their roles. In addition, a good library of online journals and industry reports was also created. This made it easy for employees to know what was happening in the industry and learn more deeply in their area. Employees were also trained in techniques related to idea generation, creativity etc. By equipping the employees with relevant knowledge, the intervention team inculcated the requisite knowledge to build an innovative culture. Now what was required was a spark.

Creating sparks through competitions

The next intervention focused on inciting employees to think differently. This was done through white paper contests. Contests focused on emerging technical themes in the areas where the organization worked. All the employees were motivated to join the contests, the intention being to ensure all employees got an experience of paper writing and the related experience of researching. Academicians were invited to give sessions on paper writing, how to structure papers, and approaches to literature review. The paper contests pushed employees to research in their area of interest and evolve their own viewpoints. Access to top journals had a positive influence on the way employees wrote papers and they also got exposed to the latest developments in the field. The paper contest participation level was very high with almost 70 percent of employees participating. The reward was monetary and employees were also informed that the best ideas in the papers would also be considered for patenting. The contests created a buzz in the organization. Since papers could be co-authored, it also helped in promoting a culture of collaboration.

Patent sessions and rewards programs

To create awareness about patents, the patent attorney was brought from the US office. The attorney gave a series of sessions on patenting, the patenting processes, how to identify patentable ideas etc. Employees were also informed about the rewards program, where rewards were given to inventors whose idea got patented. Along with this a "Wall of Fame" was built in one of the office spaces, and innovation and inventors were celebrated. Short write-ups of some of the prolific inventors were shared through the Wall. The innovators also facilitated town halls when senior leaders from the global R&D team visited. This helped in inculcating a sense of pride among the innovators and gave employees someone to look up to from their own circle.

Patent support team

To support the patent program, an in-house patent team was formed, consisting of employees who had filed for patent. They were trained in higher concepts of patenting by the patent attorney. Their role was to be innovation promoters and included facilitating idea generation, idea sniffing and exploring opportunities for ideas. The innovators would have one-on-one sessions with employees who wanted support in idea generation. Idea sniffers would sit with innovators and help them identify any innovative ideas that they had. The patent support team played an important role in promoting innovation as they were easily available for the employees and their experience of patenting helped aspiring innovators.

All these interventions had a positive impact, and the center saw a spurt of ideas generated by the employees. In a span of three years, the center became one of the most prolific innovating centers.

Aside from the reward mechanism, the rest of the interventions were focused on knowledge generation, sharing, and collaboration. The focus was on opening up the silos and enabling the flow of knowledge, inculcating knowledge through right skilling, providing access to knowledge sources and then training on innovation techniques. The contests and rewards mechanism then helped put these skills in practice.

The approach adopted included a combination of:

- Promoting sharing and collaboration;
- Building a knowledge base of journal publication and industry reports;
- Training programs on emerging technologies;
- Awareness session on patenting;
- Rewards program to incentivize patenting behavior; and
- Building support groups.

Innovating as a task and continuously improving on it

Knowledge plays a key role in creating innovation and hence it is important to understand and leverage knowledge-based interventions to sustain an innovation culture. One can have a combination of both the approaches, where an innovation culture leads to quality idea generation and an innovation program, which effectively converts these ideas into solutions.

Innovation can be managed and practiced in a planned manner, the way we manage any other function. What is required for organizations is to build deep knowledge and understanding on how this gets done. Every idea to an innovation journey should be analyzed and understood, and learning should be generated. Every idea to solution journey should be considered as a task, involving employees and processes. Every time the task is performed, focused analysis should be done about the journey. The insights generated should be ploughed back and the next journey should consider these lessons learned. These learnings should be used to create an organization-specific approach to innovation. As the organization goes through multiple cycles of idea to solution, the knowledge base of how to move from idea to solution should be enriched. After some time, an organization will realize that it has made innovating itself as its core competency. Innovating will become easy for such an organization. It will slowly start moving from innovation as an art to innovation as a science. The organization will be able to predict by when the innovative solution will be developed, what kind of team should be built, and the nature of support it will require.

Similarly, when the aim is to create an innovative culture, it should always be focused on specific areas, which can be technology or industry related. Organizations should not focus on building an organization-wide, innovation culture, but build with focus on a specific area and with a clear goal, which will give them more control into creating many regions of innovation. This will also help in replicating the same approach across multiple domains, technology, or area of working. Organizations will then approach the creation of an innovation culture as a task, which can be easily managed as a science, not as an esoteric activity, where one always waits for a pleasant accident.

Chapter 6:

How to share knowledge in the future workplace

By Clare Harman Clark, senior professional support lawyer, Taylor Wessing

Perhaps we should have seen it coming. Sixty years ago, in *The Landmarks of Tomorrow*, Peter Drucker, the thought-leader father of management philosophy, wrote convincingly about the coming age of the knowledge worker. True enough, the white-collar worker who thinks for a living prospered in the 20th century. Lawyers, engineers, and scientists attained increasing importance (and remuneration) while blue collar workers were left to face a relentless onslaught of production automation. We got comfortable, but it couldn't last. Fast forward to the current century and *Industry 4.0* – the fourth industrial revolution – is bringing new challenges to the door of the knowledge worker, who must be ready to meet its new demands in order to maximize its opportunities.

Industry 4.0 is nothing short of a sea change in the way business is run across the planet. Shorthand for process automation and data exchange, it is taking no prisoners. At first glance, the odds for businesses are not great. A telling report made to the World Economic Forum in January 2019 found that fewer than 10 percent of companies think their current business model will survive the new industrial revolution. Staring down the barrel at data-driven digital platforms, this means that over 90 percent of companies need to optimize their business models for productivity. As the report's authors Torrence and Staeritz[1] conclude, they need to look at how they create value for customers and capture value for themselves. They need to critically appraise their propositions, products, resources, processes, revenue streams, and cost structures, to make sure they are ready.

For many struggling to engage meaningfully with data analytics, or robotics, it is still early days, but the knock-on effects of Industry 4.0 are already being felt in a very physical way. The millennial isn't just inheriting the earth, it is fundamentally redesigning the workplace. Traditional landlords are seeing increasing pressure to recalibrate traditional office lets for co-working or flexible leasing terms. Companies want floor plate space that flexes with their needs and their workforces, which themselves are working in more flexible ways. Desk occupancy, the source of a major overhead for many companies, waxes and wanes as people take advantage of secure applications to work remotely, at different times of the day. Already it is virtually inconceivable that anyone who has experienced this flexibility will be easily lured back into a static, commute-heavy nine-to-five – what a way to earn a living!

The working assumption is that fast adaptors to Industry 4.0 and fast followers will emerge victorious from the revolution, and it is difficult to underestimate the role of knowledge management in this. Commentators question the future viability of those businesses that refuse to budge, like those sceptics standing stubbornly before the loom, the lightbulb, and the mainframe. But it's not just about refusing the change, or taking comfort in decades-old behaviors, it's also about being equipped to maximize the opportunities, financially and intellectually. And at the heart of this is the need to harness, articulate, and maximize a firm's key asset – its knowledge.

For the purposes of this chapter, we will consider the new tools and opportunities unleashed by Industry 4.0 that might speak to the development of traditional operation of knowledge management. In practice, the workstream generally constitutes harvesting, managing, and sharing an entire bandwidth of useful information, from the tacit experience of individuals, to academic understanding, through to the competitive advantages available in horizon and market scanning.

Pride and professionalization

The profession of knowledge management as we know it is changing. There is a convincing narrative around the need for standardization in an industry specialism that individuals have been making an art of for decades. It is about supporting the knowledge professional but also articulating the value and centricity of effective knowledge management process as firms position themselves within Industry 4.0.

As Drucker himself might have put it, the first stage to this exercise might be a *planned abandonment of yesterday's successes*, whereby the firm is emboldened to ditch the existing strategies of knowledge sharing that are no longer useful in the modern workplace. In truth, of course, many of us cling to procedures and checklists that didn't necessarily work effectively in the first place. A directory of experts is only useful when it is up-to-date, and the expert concerned isn't out of the office. Knowledge industries habitually wedded to the CPD hour may, for example, need convincing to see that training sessions can come in bite-size chunks, or delivered flexibly in order to optimize the attention span of their busy target. And while companies have long struggled with succession planning, there are new tech-enabled ways to capture knowledge across the lifetime of a job role, not just as the incumbent shuffles on. In this situation, it's not just about replicating a skill set after all; few workplaces are able genuinely via a handover note to capture a full download of an individual's passive, embedded knowledge and experience.

Identifying deficiencies makes a compelling case for moving forward, and there are industry-wide moves afoot to codify the processes of knowledge capture and share. Most recently, the release of ISO 30401:2018 *Knowledge Management Systems* in 2018 refocused attention on the process of professional standardization. It is adaptive, enabling KM teams across different industries to benchmark their own processes and competencies against a list of *should haves*. The aim is to avoid a box-ticking exercise but uses guiding principles and requirements to create a deeper understanding of quality management. It is not possible to achieve formal accreditation pursuant to the ISO, but rather it sets out 54 instances of "a company shall" to support an internal audit.

Tech and sensibility

By 2025, those millennials born between about 1980 and 2000 are forecast to comprise 75 percent of the global workforce, and this first generation of genuinely tech-savvy workers are creating real impetus for change. Millennials are more comfortable with tech – they have lots of it already in their homes and pockets – and firms needing to look to attract and retain talent must acknowledge that it will come from a pool that communicates differently, collaborates more willingly, and demands flexibility.

The flexibility part is especially key and Industry 4.0 is heralding a dramatic change in the physical office. In many workplaces, presenteeism has (finally) had its day as working patterns are personalized and businesses mandate that efficient desk occupancy relies on a revolving carousel of office attendance. In sectors such as real estate, tech is generating a change in our established, documented models. Just think about the WeWork revolution versus the traditional 15-year office space lease. Seeking flexibility and turnkey space, many businesses are looking for ease of contracting too. They want smart contracts (essentially those computer protocols intended to digitally facilitate, verify, or enforce contract negotiation or performance). They want mobile apps that enable them to review and commit to flexible licenses quickly, not enter a protracted debate leading to a comprehensive lease deed.

In this physical environment, knowledge management can make effective use of tech to support employees, assisting wellbeing in the office while increasing productivity. When offices provide IOT-enabled connected furnishings that allow employees to charge their phones via the sofas, for example, reliance on hard copy print outs to do things in the way they have always been done, can feel really clunky. As work is literally undertaken more flexibly, from the office or the home or even the coffee shop, a federated search facility of a firm's resources is vital – even better, an enterprise search facility that combines external knowledge resources that inform business decisions.

If a user cannot gain sufficient virtual overview of the knowledge tools available, many will be rendered useless. In an ever-interconnected world, an ability to see beyond discrete practice areas or departments is vital, so that information pieces can be properly organized and repurposed; drawing those dots across decentralized models to ensure that one department is talking effectively to another. From an employee perspective, it has to feel as though a library or an information services team is travelling with you.

There is a burgeoning (and often confusing) market of off-the-shelf tools designed to address the particular concerns anticipated in the future of work. Many of these speak to the difficulty of collating and sharing knowledge and maintaining brand strength across what often amounts to a physically disparate workforce. Content and contract management systems allow key documents and lessons learned to be stored accessibly and shared easily. These are not new per se – the knowledge manager has acted as in-house librarian for a long time – but these newer, more complex, content management systems offer portals and data visualization packages that can add real value, provided effective taxonomies are used. And where these taxonomies were first created and tagged manually, they can now be attributed by machine learning.

Document automation – the electronic assembly process that turns a series of transaction-specific questions into a tailored template – has also been available for decades but its take up is now mandatory in corporates focused on sustainable processes, with brands that value product consistency, where a document made by one employee must look and feel like that created by any other. A new generation of document production and data mining products employ artificial intelligence, and it is here that the direst predictions exist for the knowledge industry.

Clearly there is value in making analytic insights, sharing real-time data feeds to enable business processes to adapt, but in seeking to get *better*, past lessons suggest that this means firms trading on automated knowledge can also get *leaner*. Robotic paralegals, for example, that scan and interpret document texts, boast of error rates that far undermine the capacity of the task-tired human brain, at speeds that fundamentally challenge tried and tested fees assumptions. This is possibly the greatest challenge to the knowledge worker from Industry 4.0, and, faced with the data-driven digitization that Drucker could not have foreseen, it is important and not impossible for firms to equip their staff effectively to withstand intact the onslaught lumbering over the horizon.

Standing in the face of AI automation isn't easy. There is an emotional cost to uncertainty. Change and disruption is always hard, and for a significant part of the knowledge workforce it's especially anxiety-inducing when cloaked in unfamiliar language. Undoubtedly however, the key to positive and active engagement with new tech is knowledge-led management. While the billable hour reigns supreme in the legal industry, for example, it is possible to explain to clients that automation is merely processing the input information in order to free up valuable time; giving lawyers the space to flourish and focus on the skills for real value add – the creation of current and future transaction leverage.

In the context of this continued tech take-up, knowledge workers are a future proofing asset, not a balance sheet liability. Proactive knowledge management can identify genuine technological and data requirements from within a team so that the solutions employed create genuine business optimization, going beyond novelty. With a privileged helicopter view of team workflows, born in the legal world at least from their role as the traditional keepers of a firm's precedent bank, knowledge managers can ease a product introduction and encourage the sharing of information within it for capture.

Most importantly, in areas such as law again, such employees can ensure that the capital of knowledge is retained, ensuring the sustainability of the business model over the longer term. Junior associates in a law firm cannot afford to hand over tasks to the machines wholesale, for example, or they risk missing out on a key part of their professional development. No lawyer comes fully formed – the insight clients pay handsomely for in later qualification years has generally been hard won over years of deal experience and close document analysis in data rooms. Moreover, a firm's knowledge is worth nothing if it is not continually subject to a feedback loop, whereby it is captured, interpreted, observed, stress-tested, and upgraded. In this sense, knowledge managers are key to defending a business' future strength.

Collaboration and flexibility

Curating and maintaining communities of practice (CoPs) for knowledge-sharing has never been a mean feat. On a very human level, many knowledge workers are not naturally collaborative, and may be resistant to the creation of a collaboration platform that might package their specialist skill for anyone to use. Assuming the knowledge manager has achieved sufficient buy-in to bring people together and provide an opportunity for intercompany learning, there are always difficulties posed by clashing diaries, distances, or time zones. With the right technology, however, communities can be linked electronically and flexibly without the need for ad hoc encounters at the water cooler.

Industries like law are essentially services that have thrived on relationships and knowledge sharing and will necessarily continue to do so. Lessons learned in tech-enabled, quasi-formal CoPs are vital here. While millennials work differently, they also communicate differently. For a generation used to making plans and building social networks on nimble group-enabling apps such as WhatsApp, the formal email chains still preferred by most offices seem as antiquated as snake on a Nokia mobile. Indeed, the inbox is about the only piece of 40-year-old tech you are likely to use today. Understanding how to talk in a firm but on the go is clearly at the heart of understanding how to manage the communications between the company and the rest of the world, as it is at the heart of sharing knowledge effectively.

The argument is further assisted as a large number of services are being commoditized. The first port of call for a prickly rash is likely Google, not a doctor. Your common or garden law firm, meanwhile, is no longer the sole gatekeeper to The Law. In this industry, the atomization of legal services has seen a growth in online marketplaces for sharing legal self-help, and if we do not find a way as an industry of creating best practice and transaction efficiencies together, of articulating the value in collaboration, our clients will do it for us. With their minds firmly on the consequences of Industry 4.0 on their own digital platforms, they will dictate the tech tools their lawyers and other members of their supply chain should use to create efficiencies.

It is tempting to respond quickly to Industry 4.0. If you want to go fast, as the saying goes, go alone. But most of us like to think we are here for the long haul and management consultants will tell you that to go far, you go together. Sharing knowledge in the future will mean being honest about the value of tech tools to make efficiencies in the low hanging fruit of knowledge creation. And as the take up of these new products is likely to become key to client experience and retention, it makes perfect sense to have clients on any tech innovation steering committee for the firm.

Conclusion

The challenges of the future workplace are not just about flexing demands on bricks and mortar office space, or even the need to install IoT-enabled connected furnishings, or shoehorn tech into established processes. Rather, demands for different kinds of flexible working, across multiple locations, have given a new centricity to knowledge management within firms keen to ensure the efficient sharing and retaining of their corporate's learning, as well as its talent. Finding innovative KM strategies for this brave new world, ways that respond most effectively to Industry 4.0 and its demand for data-driven digital platforms, will prove key to legitimizing ourselves and our service. In fact, it's probably the only way to survive.

Reference

1. Torrance. S., and F. Staeritz, 15 January 2019. www.weforum.org/agenda/2019/01/is-your-business-model-fit-for-the-fourth-industrial-revolution/

Chapter 7:
What should KM actually *do*?

By Caroline White-Robinson, Head of L&D, Shoosmiths

Should KM be focused on the capture and sharing of knowledge, or could it create greater opportunities by designing, developing, and delivering processes, structure, and behavior related to stimulating learning and optimizing processes for harnessing knowledge as it emerges? This chapter looks at how KM can be a relevant, just-in-time and emergent function within any law firm. I'm going to discuss how I think KM sits at the hub of the organizational wheel and its potential impact on operational effectiveness and people.

We're going through changes

Change is the only constant we can grip hold of. How KM leads the way in addressing change can either be done proactively or reactively. I believe that KM should be part of the mechanism of and for change. To achieve this, everyone in a KM team needs to believe that they are a leader. Easier said than done, but if a growth mindset can be established early on – i.e. KM has an active part to play in the delivery of strategy – stakeholders and users of the outputs generated by KM will bring KM in at a much earlier stage when addressing change and all that it brings with it.

People are often stuck when it comes to change – not knowing what change is required or how to change being the two biggest challenges.

> *"If I had asked people what they wanted, they would have said faster horses."*
> Henry Ford

If placed at the hub of the organizational wheel in any knowledge business, KM has the opportunity to be an ambassador for change. Constantly thinking about how it adds value in an evolving organization, it must be a role model for change, demonstrating a living and breathing strategy that moves with the changing dynamics of employee engagement, client needs, and regulatory demands. KM should bring the "collective clever" of a business together so that it might develop innovative solutions based on the knowledge within its business and prepare itself for the challenges and changes ahead. This chapter outlines how KM can do this through the use of appreciative enquiry, business improvement across operations, development of wisdom and harnessing experience in a learning culture, and the need for strong feedback loops.

The role of KM has and must change over time as the requirements of the businesses we work in demand new ways of thinking and operating. Where once just having a mobile phone was aspirational it is now considered an everyday part of life (business as usual) and it is now being developed to be a payment device, camera, and document storage device – to name but a few functions. KM must do the same and move away from just capturing (document management systems are the graveyards we consign information and knowledge to) and begin sharing knowledge with an aim of adding extra value by developing more functionality, improved performance, and ultimately excellent client service within the business. This means that as a function it must find its way into areas such as innovation teams, business improvement discussions, client experience discussions, and development of an information systems (IS) architecture that will act as an enabler for change.

So what kind of areas should KM be thinking about having an impact on?

Client experience

If it is a knowledge business then the chances are that clients want to pay for the knowledge in a way that suits them. Therefore, how firms bespoke knowledge to each client should be top of the list, and so knowledge management teams should know how their activities contribute to the client experience.

Knowledge management should aim to bring the collective clever of its organization together; therefore enhancing the solution presented to the client and effectively the experience the client has.

Knowledge management should also facilitate the speed at which knowledge can be assimilated in real time across locations, time zones and cultural barriers, ultimately supporting an efficient and timely service to clients.

What is the business rationale for this?

Figure 1: How knowledge impacts organizations.

The feedback that can be gathered as a result of how and what knowledge is used within the business can have a dramatic effect on what the culture looks like. For example, if senior managers always claim the intellectual property of those around them, where is the incentive for employees to keep giving their best work? Over the long-term this will have an effect on the people and attrition rates will rise, the quality of work reduces, and client experience is damaged.

Knowledge management must be fit for purpose itself in order to help the organization be fit for purpose. Businesses will no longer be fit for purpose if they remain a matrix organization, where information and data flows from the top to the bottom. The speed at which data and information is shared is faster than it has ever been, the origins of the information can be varied and vast in nature, and the way it is stored means it needs to be assessed at an instant if we are to fulfil the next generations' need for self-service knowledge and wisdom. The next generation want to be empowered through what they know and how they can add value; KM should be instrumental in providing this in a way that boosts positive employee engagement. The way in which the next generation give feedback also needs to fit into the way in which businesses collect the "collective clever" which goes into making years' worth of expertise. Just think of Trip Advisor and your ability to rate the use of an app by using the "star" rating scale. Immediate, honest, and accessible.

Knowledge management has got to be part of the decision-making process when it comes to knowledge-based decision-making. Knowledge management professionals must build enough gravitas within their organizations, demonstrating that they understand the strategic direction as well as being able to communicate how knowledge management supports this.

In the leadership world the term VUCA has been coined. The acronym describes the world in which we work as being volatile, uncertain, complex, and ambiguous. This means making decisions is harder than it ever has been and a trusted source of "collective clever" is a valuable commodity. Therefore in this new world, knowledge management should be valued more, rather than consigned to the corridors of a back room function, simply storing and organizing information.

Delivering what clients want

Clients want law firms to be able to collaborate more effectively, work as a wider team on matters, and to share their experience to ensure the very best outcome for the situation. Employees will be required to "jump" on and off project teams and learn the dynamics of building trust in teams quickly in order to be effective. It is well known that, without trust, people won't share their most valuable resource – knowledge.

Know what your people want – to trust others and to be trusted

How can knowledge management support a culture of trust? It is important that all KM professionals take an active interest in organizational design (OD) or indeed seek out the person in their law firm who is responsible for OD. Understanding the levers within the organization that will inevitably build or undermine trust is the first step in building a learning culture supportive of business improvement. Often this might fall under the remit of the HRD but in many firms the role will lie with the L&D team. If this is the case it provides a useful insight into what employees need and want from their employer from a development perspective but also demonstrate what they are prepared to share with their employer. The training given by professional support lawyers and development teams should feedback into the KM team their findings on the areas that are being challenged or that are challenging, and KM should work with wider stakeholders to ensure that employees have everything they need to be able to fulfil their greatest potential. One of the biggest sources of disengagement across workforces is the lack of opportunity and development. KM can help lead the way in this space by making it easy for employees to learn new knowledge. But should it just be knowledge? With the advent of YouTube it is easier than ever to demonstrate both knowledge and skills in an immediate, honest, and accessible way – just take the success of TED talks.

Knowledge is like water; given the opportunity it has the potential to run through everything. The feedback below was given as part of a client listening exercise. It shows just how clients expect employees to behave.

> *"We love a spanner. Someone who spans out, learns something new or innovative, finds out what's going on outside the business then comes back and teaches it, champions it within our business. Encourage and embrace your spanners."*

KM should be the ambassador for those spanners. Constantly learning, constantly feeding back, constantly engaging with our workforce and clients.

Business improvement in a learning culture

Business process improvement (BPI) is a management exercise in which business leaders use various methodologies to analyze their processes and procedures to identify areas where they can improve accuracy, effectiveness and/or efficiency and then redesign those processes to realize the improvements. Business process improvement works by identifying the operations or employee skills that could be improved to encourage smoother procedures, more efficient workflow and overall business growth.

If we look at BPI in the context of a learning culture, the power of the two combined is quite compelling. Matthew Syed's book *Black Box Thinking*[1] outlines what it takes to create a culture where it is encouraged to learn and to fail. Taking inspiration from the aviation industry, the method of "black box thinking" encourages individuals to constantly review their performance, highlighting what they could do differently to reduce errors and mistakes, just like the black box produces feedback on how the pilots have performed.

By identifying areas that can be improved, this knowledge can be fed back into the operations to help improve operations management and with new insights being fed into innovation groups to support a design thinking process.

Positioning KM as the hub of the organizational wheel is the first step in creating the value that can be truly delivered through a joined up strategy, connecting knowledge with improvement within a learning culture.

Reference

1. *Black Box Thinking*, Matthew Syed, John Wiley, 2015.

Chapter 8: Driving innovation through communities

By Vincent Ribiere, Ph.D., The Institute for Knowledge and Innovation Southeast Asia (IKI-SEA), Bangkok University – Thailand

Introduction

Innovation is defined by the American Society for Quality (2018) as "the successful conversion of new concepts and knowledge into new products, services, or processes that deliver new customer value in the marketplace". As we can see from this definition, and from many others, innovation doesn't come in a vacuum, nor from an "Aha/Eureka" moment; it comes from the process of converting, connecting, mixing, or rearranging knowledge in a novel way. So, the raw material for innovation is knowledge and novel ways of combining it. Consequently, it is very important for organizations to properly manage their knowledge asset/capital if they want to be able to systematically innovate. The reality is that, even though we have been talking about the benefits of properly managing knowledge in an organization since the late 1980s[1] (through the discipline of Knowledge Management), very few organizations have implemented and sustained a systematic way of doing so. Does your organization know what it knows? Can it provide you with a detailed list of all knowledge domains, domain experts, and knowledge assets it possesses? Does it know what its critical knowledge is? Can it also provide you with a list of what it doesn't know? Demonstrating that it has clearly identified what it needs to know in order to achieve its strategy/objective, and that it has identified its knowledge gaps and the learning actions to fill them up. Based on our experience, few organizations are capable of doing so, which leads to a lot of inefficiencies, of having to re-invent the wheel and, in the context of this book, leads to inefficient and non-systematic ways of innovating, since knowledge, the raw material for innovation, is not properly identified and managed!

Being able to properly identify what an organization knows is the first step towards creating an environment that fosters innovation, but it is not sufficient; knowledge needs to flow in the organization to be leveraged and to be the source of new knowledge creation and innovation. This is also a very old concept that was introduced in the mid-1990s by Professors Nonaka and Takeuchi through their well-known SECI Model.[2] They present that the flow and conversion of knowledge from Tacit to Explicit through the four conversions activities – Socialization (tacit to tacit), Externalization (tacit to explicit), Combination (explicit to explicit) and Internationalization (explicit to tacit) – is the source of new knowledge creation. Consequently, organizations need to have in place some tools, mechanisms, and practices to support each of these four conversions activities, so knowledge flows and triggers the generation of new knowledge.

Organizations already have in their hands a part of the recipe to make innovation happen – identifying what they know and making sure this knowledge is shared and transferred across the organization so it can lead to new ideas and new knowledge creation. This flow of knowledge should not be limited to the internal knowledge of the organization; external knowledge should also be screened, captured and disseminated.

What roles do communities play in supporting these previously defined knowledge flow activities? This is what this chapter will explain in detail.

Communities

Communities of practice

Organizations are naturally composed of various types of communities. The most popular are Communities of Interests and Communities of Practice, but they might be called differently in different organizations, such as Learning groups (HP), Family groups (Xerox), Peer groups (BP), Knowledge networks (IBM), CoPs (Caterpillar), Techs Clubs (Chrysler), Knowledge Silos Breakers (World Bank), etc.

The concept of Communities of Practice (CoPs) was coined by Etienne Wenger[3] in 1998 who defines it as "groups of people who share a concern or a passion for something they do and learn how to do it better as they interact regularly". CoPs are informal and voluntary groups of people interested in the same topic/problem who join to learn from each other and to develop their community and tools. They are often led by subject matter experts and can operate by meeting physically and/or virtually. It is highly encouraged that members of the CoP come from different business units, so diversity of thoughts, ideas, and approaches can emerge for community activities. Different members might have different responsibilities among the CoP (champions, experts, facilitators, integrators, members, as well as lurkers). The main objectives of a CoP's activities are social learning, problem solving, and knowledge sharing.

Gongla and Rizzuto presented a model of CoP evolution in 2001,[4] where communities evolve through five stages, as presented in Figure 1. When CoPs reach their more mature stage (adaptive stage), they are able to generate new knowledge and to innovate and it is at this stage when they are more likely to act as Communities of Innovation (CoI). We will explain in the next sections how and why.

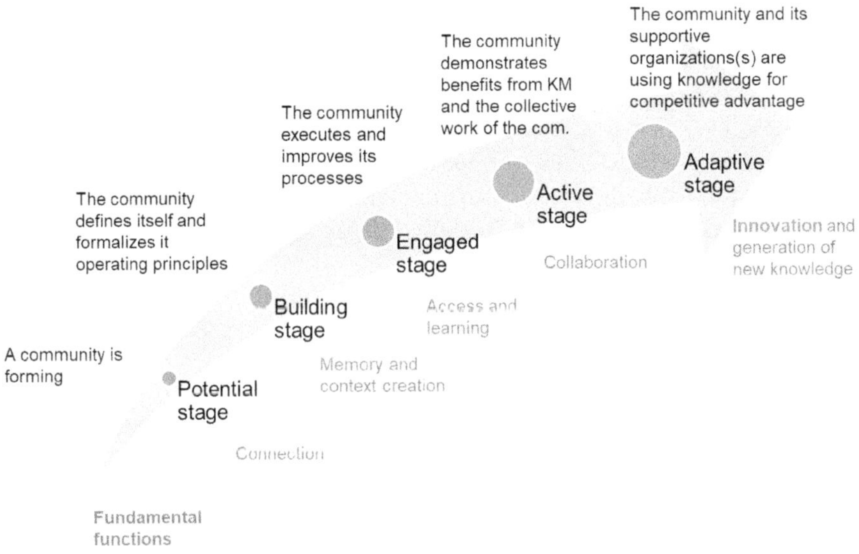

Figure 1: CoP evolution stages based on Gongla and Rizzuto.

The 2019 findings of the state of community management report, conducted every year by the Community Roundtable[5] among international organizations, show that the top three CoP business outcomes connected to community value are:

- Culture and organizational change – 61 percent;
- Quality improvement – 50 percent; and
- Innovation – 47 percent (reemphasizing the role that CoPs can play in innovation).

Communities of Innovation

Communities of Innovation (CoIs) are a matured form of Communities of Practice with a particular interest in supporting innovation. CoIs are groups made up of motivated individuals working together towards a common goal, not because of orders from their superiors, but because they are convinced of their common cause. CoIs are driven by innovation champions and their social networks.[6] CoIs are safe places for the creation, improvement, validation and support of innovatory ideas.

Lim and Ong compare CoPs to CoIs in Table 1. We do agree with this comparison when it comes to relatively young CoPs, but when it comes to more mature CoPs, the CoP listed attributes might merge with the CoI attributes, or subgroups of mature CoPs might join to pursue a particular innovation project/challenge that their community is facing.

CoIs have demonstrated their capacity for improving the value creation process.[7] Sarazin, Simon and Cohendet[8] have collected a series of success case studies of how various types and forms of CoIs have played an important role in various Canadian and French companies (such as Ubisoft, Salomon, Decathlon, Renault, Michelin, Schneider Electric, SEB Group, etc.).

	CoP	CoI
Epistemology	Learning	Innovating
Nature	Emergent (natural)	Maybe emergent (natural) or cultivated (artificial)
Lifespan	Longer	Shorter
Purpose	Broader	Narrower
Scope	Single function	Maybe single function or cross-functional
Participants	Volunteers	Maybe volunteers or conscripts
Number of participants	Few to many	Few

Level of trust between participants	Low to moderate	High
Cost to participants	Low to moderate	High
Benefit to organization	Low to moderate	High
Motivation to join	Personal interest	Personal or organizational

Table 1: The differences between Communities of Practice and Communities of Innovation.[9]

Innovation

We previously provided a definition of innovation, but there are different ways to look at innovation. Keeley, L. et al.[10] classify innovation in 10 types:

- Process (Enabling process, Core process);
- Offering (Product performance, Product system, Service);
- Delivery (Channel, Brand, Customer experience); and
- Finance (Business model, networking).

Based on this taxonomy we can see that innovation belongs to every business activity and it is not just the responsibility of R&D, Marketing or of the New Product Development team. Innovation has become the responsibility of everyone in the organization. By involving members from various business units to join CoIs to collaboratively innovate, the innovation outputs might offer a higher value proposition.

For this chapter we will focus on the differences between incremental and breakthrough (radical).[11] An incremental innovation will enhance existing offerings or will improve internal operations or will rely on adopting/deploying a breakthrough technology. A breakthrough (radical) innovation will help reaching new customer segments, or new markets, or developing new business models, or providing radical new ways of operating and working or adopting/deploying a disruptive technology. This second type of innovation can generate more value to the organization but it is also the most difficult and risky to achieve.

Ceserani[12] presents the cycling worlds model (Figure 2) that he describes as "The challenge for leaders is to maintain supportive and entrepreneurial climates in the operational world in order to maintain the business of today, and to help people build and use their skills and capabilities to be creative and innovative in order to create the business of tomorrow".

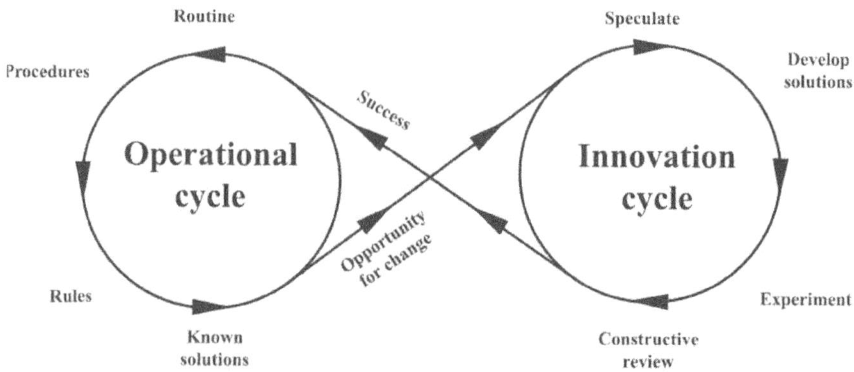

Figure 2: The cycling worlds model.

This model clearly illustrates the need to balance the routine work and its challenges (left side), usually solved by incremental innovation solutions, and looking for novel solutions to break the routines (right side), usually solved by more radical types of innovation. This model can also be used to understand the need to manage past knowledge (operational cycle) but at the same time to look for new knowledge (innovation cycle). In his innovation ambidexterity model, March[13] emphasizes the need for organizations to balance their Exploitation (Using know-how) and Exploration (Gaining know-how) activities in order to learn and innovate. In general, CoPs primarily support the Exploitation aspect (operational aspect), since they are mainly conducted internally in the organization but in order to support the Exploration aspect (innovation cycle), and turn into CoIs, CoPs need to achieve a high level of maturity (as depicted in Figure 1), be "innoverse", and must have attained a certain level of collaboration by integrating with social networks communities. The following sections will explain in detail these two additional important aspects.

Innoversity

In order for CoPs to turn into CoIs, a certain number of factors need to be in place. Justesen[14] proposes the concept of Innoversity (Innovation

Diversity) where CoPs are likely to be more innovative if they embrace the following five drivers:

- Absorptive capacity[15] – the ability to recognize the value of new, external information, assimilate it and apply it;
- Requisite variety – variety in techne and cognition that will lead to the ability to control discontinuities/perturbations;
- Network variety – ability to tap into broad networks of contacts;
- Creative destruction[16] – being willing to destroy the old in the heart of innovation and the means to profits; and
- Problem solving – diversity of perspectives and points of views.

These drivers are driven by the composition of the CoP members as well as by their mindset, openness, and diverse background. In 2012, Google launched the "Aristotle project" in order to identify what factors needed to be present to create the "perfect" team at Google.[17] After studying all factors that they believed could have an influence (i.e., How often did teammates socialize outside the office? Did they have the same hobbies? Were their educational backgrounds similar? Was it better for all teammates to be outgoing or for all of them to be shy? etc.), no patterns could be identified showing that a mix of specific personality types or skills or backgrounds made any difference. A team of psychologists and sociologists looked at what team norms/behaviors mattered the most. They discovered that "team psychological safety" was the main factor that made team members feel comfortable and trust each other. The concept of team psychological safety was coined by Professor Amy Edmondson[18] and can be defined as "a shared belief that the team is safe for interpersonal risk taking" and could be further described as:

"Team psychological safety is not the same as group cohesiveness, as research has shown this can reduce willingness to disagree and challenge others' views, such as in the phenomenon of groupthink, implying a lack of interpersonal risk taking. The term is meant to suggest neither a careless sense of permissiveness, nor an unrelenting positive affect but, rather, a sense of confidence that the team will not embarrass, reject or punish someone for speaking up."

Amy Edmonson and Google both found in their separate studies that the teams that made more mistakes were actually more successful. Creating an environment in which people feel comfortable to take risks is key to fostering innovative workplaces.

Even though "team psychological safety" was studied in the context of teams, it positively affects CoPs and CoIs in the same manner.[19 20]

Expanding the levels of CoP/CoI Collaboration

CoPs can operate face-to-face or virtually. Most CoPs currently use collaborative platforms, discussion groups, and content management repositories to store and share their documents. Most of these collaborative platforms also now offer a social media interface to facilitate interactions between members. They mainly follow what Cook[21] introduced as the four Cs of Enterprise 2.0, which are Connection, Collaboration, Communication and Cooperation.

- Communication – communication platforms are those that allow people to converse with others, either by text, image, voice or video, or a combination of these;
- Cooperation – sharing software enables people to share content with others in structured and unstructured ways;
- Collaboration – collaboration tools encourage people to collaborate with each other on particular problems, directly and indirectly in both central and distributed ways; and
- Connection – networking technologies make it possible for people to make connections with and between both content and other people.

Similarly, Coleman presents the different levels of collaboration, adding two basic initial levels that are also supported by social technologies – Conversation and Coordination. Such collaborative features are important for CoPs to share knowledge, learn from each other, and to solve problems. In order for CoPs to become CoIs, we would like to propose two additional collaboration dimensions also starting with the letter "C", which are Co-creation/design, and Crowdsourcing (Figure 3).

Referring back to March's innovation ambidexterity model, CoPs and the traditional 6Cs Social Technologies features primarily support the Exploitation aspect, since they are mainly conducted internally in the organization. In order to support the Exploration aspect, CoPs and CoIs need to open up and internal social technologies need to integrate with external social networks.

Figure 4 presents how the integration of internal corporate social media platforms with external social media platforms could be a source

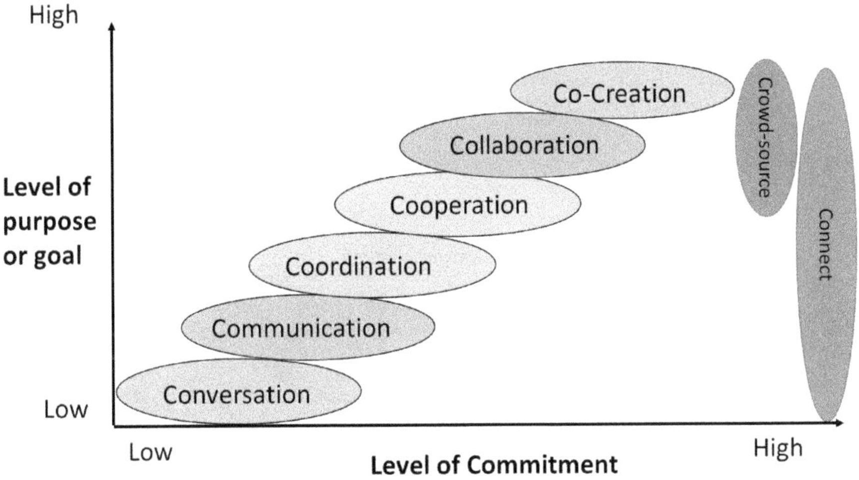

Figure 3: Levels of collaboration (8Cs), extended from Coleman.[22]

of co-production of knowledge, social learning and innovation (CoP/CoI innovation ecosystem). Usually, CoPs use the 6Cs social technologies (Conversation, Communication, Coordination, Cooperation, Collaboration, and Connection) to collaborate inward, for example a CoP can have its own corporate collaborative platform involving only its CoP members and/or other relevant business units (1). At the next level, the CoP might want to start collaborating outward by opening-up and interacting with its external environment (Customers, Experts, Partners and Suppliers, Professional networks) (2) by sharing experience, ideas, lessons learned, best practices, etc. In return, it will expect to gain new ideas, opinions, and new ties that will help it to broaden the scope of its knowledge domain and ignite its innovation opportunities. Where we believe the most potential exists is at the integration of both internal and external social technologies (3). This third level of collaboration leads to co-creation/design of solutions with actors from both internal and external environments and/or can be a platform for collective intelligence where solutions to problems can be crowdsourced.

Attaining levels 2 and 3 of collaboration will broaden the knowledge and idea horizons of CoPs and CoIs, which have a tendency to experience groupthink issues after having worked together for a long time. Such collaboration will allow them to gain knowledge and ideas from other industries and will allow them to BenchLearn and to produce some transformational innovation. It will support the weak Exploration part of the ambidextrous CoP and CoI innovation mechanism.

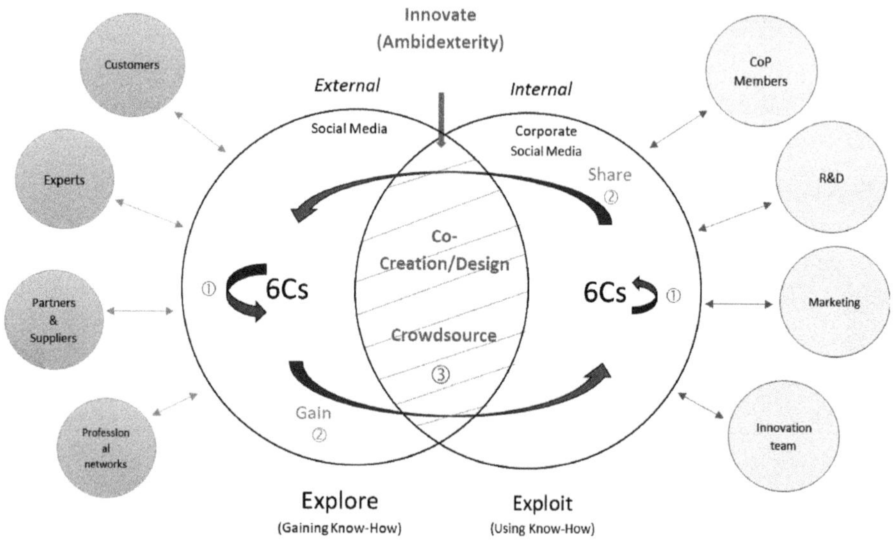

Figure 4: CoP/CoI innovation ecosystem.

As this model presents and reinforces, knowledge has to flow not only internally inside the organization from individuals, to teams and to CoPs/CoIs, but also externally. The open innovation concept[23] needs to also apply at the CoP/CoI levels if organizations want to boost their innovation engine.

Conclusion

This chapter has presented the important role that Communities, and in particular Communities of Innovation, can play in order to foster innovation in organizations. Communities do not operate in a vacuum, their organization must have in place a clear innovation strategy, an innovation governance model, strong support from leadership, a culture supporting risk taking and failure, and some sort of recognition mechanism for innovative behaviors. Such communities must also be properly facilitated in order to be sustainable. The use of social technologies can support mature CoPs and CoIs to innovate by connecting them with their external environment and by integrating two new features (Co-Creation/Design and Crowdsourcing) to the traditional 6Cs so innovative ideas and the testing of these ideas can be customer/client driven. These two new features support the Exploration aspect of innovation, commonly lacking in most closed community environments (focusing on Exploitation). By further engaging in conversational and co-creation interactions with its external environment, mature CoPs and CoIs can co-produce/construct new knowledge, engage in social learning, and develop more radical types of innovation. They key here is to create and maintain these internal and external flows of knowledge that will lead to innovation.

References

1. Sveiby, K. E. (1987). *Managing Knowhow*: Bloomsbury.
2. Nonaka, I., & Takeuchi, H. (1995). *The Knowledge Creating Company*: Oxford University Press.
3. Wenger, E. (1998). *Communities of practice : learning, meaning, and identity.* Cambridge, UK; New York, NY: Cambridge University Press.
4. Gongla, P., & Rizzuto, C. R. (2001). Evolving communities of practice: IBM Global Services experience. *IBM Systems Journal, 40*(4), 842–862.
5. The Community Roundtable. (2019). *The 2019 state of community management report*. Retrieved from https://communityroundtable.com
6. Coakes, E., & Smith, P. (2007). Developing communities of innovation by identifying innovation champions. *The Learning Organization, 14*(1), 74–85.
7. Grimaldi, M., Cricelli, L., & Rogo, F. (2012). *A methodology to assess value creation in communities of innovation* (Vol. 13).
8. Sarazin, B., Simon, L., & Cohendet, P. (2017). *Les communautés d'innovation: de la liberté créatrice à l'innovation organisée*: Éditions EMS.
9. Lim, M., & Ong, B. Y. (2019). Communities of innovation. *International Journal of Innovation Science, 0*(0), null. doi:doi:10.1108/IJIS-09-2017-0086
10. Keeley, L., Walters, H., Pikkel, R., & Quinn, B. (2013). *Ten Types of Innovation: The Discipline of Building Breakthroughs*: Wiley.
11. Nagji, B., & Tuff, G. (2012). Managing Your Innovation Portfolio. *Harvard Business Review*, 90(5), 66–74.
12. Ceserani, J. (2003). *Big ideas: putting the zest into creativity and innovation at work*: Kogan Page Publishers.
13. March, J. G. (1991). Exploration and Exploitation in Organizational Learning. *Organization Science, 2*(1), 71–87.
14. Justesen, S. (2004). Innoversity in Communities of Practice. In P. Hildreth & C. Kimble (Eds.), *Knowledge Networks: Innovation through Communities of Practice*, 79–95: Idea Group Publishing.
15. Cohen, W. M., & Levinthal, D. A. (1990). Absorptive Capacity: A New Perspective on Learning and Innovation. *Administrative Science Quarterly, 35*(1), 128–152. doi:10.2307/2393553

16. Levitt, T. (1962). Innovation in marketing: *New perspectives for profit and growth*. New York: McGraw-Hill.
17. Duhigg, C. (2016). What Google learned from its quest to build the perfect team. *The New York Times Magazine, 26*, 2016.
18. Edmondson, A. C. (1999). Psychological safety and learning behavior in work teams. *Administrative Science Quarterly, 44*(2), 350–383. Edmondson, A. C. (2012). *Teaming: How organizations learn, innovate, and compete in the knowledge economy*: John Wiley & Sons. Edmondson, A. C. (2013). *Teaming to innovate*: John Wiley & Sons.
19. Kirkman, B. L., Cordery, J. L., Mathieu, J., Rosen, B., & Kukenberger, M. (2013). Global organizational communities of practice: The effects of nationality diversity, psychological safety, and media richness on community performance. *Human Relations, 66*(3), 333–362.
20. Zhang, Y., Fang, Y., Wei, K.-K., & Chen, H. (2010). Exploring the role of psychological safety in promoting the intention to continue sharing knowledge in virtual communities. *International Journal of Information Management, 30*(5), 425–436.
21. Cook, N. (2008). *Enterprise 2.0: How Social Software Will Change the Future of Work*. Aldershot, Hampshire, England: Gower Publishing Limited.
22. Coleman, D. (Producer). (2012). Starting the Collaborative Conversation. Retrieved from http://slideplayer.com/slide/7468017/
23. Chesbrough, H. (2006). *Open Innovation: The New Imperative for Creating And Profiting from Technology*: Harvard Business Press.

www.ingramcontent.com/pod-product-compliance
Ingram Content Group UK Ltd.
Pitfield, Milton Keynes, MK11 3LW, UK
UKHW021848150926
8657IPUK00005B/141

9 781783 58374